FILIPPO BERIO

THE MEDITERRANEAN
OLIVE OIL COOKBOOK

—— FILIPPO BERIO ——
THE MEDITERRANEAN
OLIVE OIL COOKBOOK

Louise Steele

VERMILION
LONDON

First published 1994

1 3 5 7 9 10 8 6 4 2

Recipes © Random House (UK) Ltd 1994
Photographs © Michelle Garrett 1994

First published in the United Kingdom in 1994 by
Vermilion
an imprint of Ebury Press
Random House, 20 Vauxhall Bridge Road, London SW1V 2SA

Random House Australia (Pty) Limited
20 Alfred Street, Milsons Point, Sydney,
New South Wales 2061, Australia

Random House New Zealand Limited
18 Poland Road, Glenfield,
Auckland 10, New Zealand

Random House South Africa (Pty) Limited
PO Box 337, Bergvlei, South Africa

Random House UK Limited Reg. No. 954009

A CIP catalogue record for this book is available from the British Library

ISBN: 0 09 178962 1

Designed by Clive Dorman
Typeset from author's disks by Clive Dorman & Co.
Printed and bound in Great Britain by Mackays of Chatham Plc, Kent

Papers used by Ebury Press are natural, recyclable products made from
wood grown in sustainable forests.

Contents

Introduction   6

The Filippo Berio Story   8

Starters and Snacks   10

Soups   20

Seafood   30

Salads   41

Chicken and Duck   51

Meats   62

Grains, Beans and Pasta   73

Vegetables   83

Barbecues   93

Microwave Recipes   103

Dressings, Sauces and Marinades   113

Flavoured Oils, Dried Tomatoes and
     Other Preserves   122

Breads   129

Cakes and Puddings   139

Index   156

Note:
Quantities are given in metric and imperial measures.
Please follow one set of measurements only as they are not
interchangeable.

Introduction

The phenomenon of a product which is nutritious, tasty and versatile, but above all healthy, has been known to olive oil users in the Mediterranean for centuries. It is only in comparatively recent years that United Kingdom consumers have discovered the reals benefits of using olive oil.

This book aims to help consumers make the most of olive oil with a nutritious and healthy selection of recipes. It also aims to reduce the mystery surrounding olive oil and to explain the various types of oil and their uses.

Extra-Virgin Olive Oil

To receive the accolade 'extra' virgin olive oil, this completely natural product of the first pressing of olives must achieve an absolutely perfect colour and flavour and have an acidity of less than 1 per cent. Of course there are ordinary virgin oils on the market, but these have a higher acidity and are, therefore, not marketed under the premium FILIPPO BERIO label.

FILIPPO BERIO offer two styles of extra-virgin olive oil: the normal high-quality Extra-Virgin Olive Oil and the premium 'Special Selection' Extra-Virgin Olive Oil for those occasions when only the best will do.

The full aroma and flavour of extra-virgin olive oil adds authenticity to a wide variety of Mediterranean cuisine, including pizza and pasta dishes, and is also ideal for dressing salads.

Pure Olive Oil

FILIPPO BERIO's reputation for quality is highlighted in the content of virgin olive oil blended with refined oil to produce Pure Olive Oil. Economies effected by using less virgin olive oil lead to cheaper, inferior products and should be avoided.

Pure Olive Oil can fulfil all the functions of extra-virgin olive oil in recipes where a less pronounced flavour is required. It may also be used as a base for home-made salad dressings, mayonnaise and marinades.

Light Olive Oil

This specially refined oil is an innovation which, with its mild flavour and light texture, has firmly established olive oil as an everyday cooking oil.

FILIPPO BERIO Mild & Light Olive Oil retains all the health benefits, whilst its high smokepoint and slower breakdown, compared to other oils, makes it ideal for either deep or shallow frying, stir-frying and baking.

Cooking with Olive Oil

Olive oils differ in quality, smokepoint, colour, flavour and aroma. Each type of olive oil has its own purpose. Genuine extra-virgin oil has the richest, deepest flavour and captures the essence of the olive itself, but isn't appropriate for every dish. Since cooking reduces the flavour of extra-virgin oil, it's a waste of money to use it in baking, sauces or recipes in which other ingredients might overpower its taste. Save it for salads and other cold dishes or trickle it over hot dishes just before serving so the rich flavour can be fully enjoyed. Use it in dishes such as pasta with oil and garlic, where it is the featured ingredient. Use milder oils in dishes where the flavour will be dominated by other ingredients. Their lighter nature allows the flavours of the food to come through, and they are usually preferred for sautéing and frying.

Cooking oils should not be allowed to smoke since the chemical structure of fats and oils is changed when heated beyond the smoking point. Olive oil, unlike seed oils, remains stable at relatively high temperatures because of its antioxidant and high oleic acid content. Pure olive oils have smoking points ranging from 207-242°C (406-468°F).

Olive oil, like wine, also offers a wide range of flavours, colours and aromas that vary with the nature of the soil and climate where the olives were cultivated and the type of olive used. In fact, olive oil is the only cooking and salad oil that offers a variety of natural flavours. These can vary from bland to peppery and can be described as mild (delicate, light and almost buttery tasting), semi-fruity (stronger with more olive taste), fruity (oil with a strong olive flavour), pizzico (oil with a peppery accent), rustic (hearty oil) and sweet.

Colours can range from delicate straw hues to emerald green. While dark, intense colour may signal a fruity flavour and lighter colours may indicate a nuttier flavour, this is not always the case since oils are often blends of several varieties of olives. Like wines, olive oils have vintages caused by changes in growing conditions that affect colour and flavour. In fact, you might buy two very green oils and discover that one is intensely peppery and the other light and fruity.

Since no two oils are alike they should be chosen as you would choose wine, by personal taste preference and budget considerations. Beware of oils that have a thick, greasy appearance or those that are thin, pallid and watery. Also avoid those that have been stored in the sun or have a copper tint.

The Filippo Berio Story...

Filippo Berio was born in Oneglia on 8 December 1829. When he was still very young, his family came to live in Lucca, an ancient walled city in Tuscany, famous for the manufacture of silk and the finest olive oil.

As a young man, Filippo Berio began to produce olive oil. The brand that bears his name first appeared in 1850. During the second half of the nineteenth century, there was a mass emigration of Italians to North America and the northern European countries. Not surprisingly, the Italians who went abroad wanted to maintain their tradition of Italian cuisine in their new homelands, and so it was that Filippo Berio became very involved in exporting his olive oil to these communities.

Over the next forty years, Filippo Berio steadily built up his business. He became famous as a great connoisseur of olive oil, personally testing and selecting the oils that would be sold under the FILIPPO BERIO brand. As a result, by the end of the nineteenth century, FILIPPO BERIO was the foremost brand of olive oil to be exported from Italy, winning many international awards for its supreme quality.

In 1891, Filippo Berio formed a partnership with Giovanni Silvestrini and FILIPPO BERIO oil became the premier export brand of the new company. When Filippo Berio died, in Lucca, in 1894, he had the satisfaction of knowing that the future of his brand was assured.

In 1910, Giovanni Silvestrini joined forces with Dino Fontana and formed a new company, Società per Azioni Lucchese Olii e Vini (SALOV), which still owns the

FILIPPO BERIO brand. Today, the business is run by the grandchildren and great-grandchildren of Dino Fontana, and remains in Lucca.

While sophisticated modern equipment is now used in the production of FILIPPO BERIO olive oil, with the strictest quality controls being carried out in computerized laboratories, Filippo Berio himself would still recognize the methods of selecting the finest oils. This process is still carried out on a daily basis by members of the Fontana family, bringing to the testing of olive oil skills that have developed over four generations.

Today, all the major olive oil producers in Italy are owned by multinational conglomerates – with one exception. SALOV remains an Italian company, and is still in family ownership. Filippo Berio would have been proud.

FILIPPO BERIO olive oil is enjoyed all over the world. In Great Britain, FILIPPO BERIO has been the best-selling brand of olive oil for more than a decade. British consumers, in ever-increasing numbers, appreciate that these high-quality olive oils will enhance the flavour of their food and form part of a balanced, healthy diet.

If you would like further product or health information concerning FILIPPO BERIO olive oil, please write to:

FILIPPO BERIO INFORMATION SERVICE
Raans Road
Amersham
Buckinghamshire HP6 6JJ

Starters and Snacks

Warm Salad of Mixed Mushrooms with Garlic Croûtons

Serves 4-6

350 g (12 oz) mixed salad leaves (such as young spinach, rocket, lamb's lettuce, curly endive)

3 slices white bread, crusts removed

40 g (1½ oz) butter

5 tablespoons extra-virgin olive oil

1 garlic clove, crushed

450 g (1 lb) mixed mushrooms, cleaned and quartered or sliced, if large

3 shallots, chopped

2 tablespoons chopped fresh chives

2 tablespoons balsamic vinegar

2 tablespoons lemon juice

1 teaspoon sugar

salt and freshly ground black pepper

shavings of Parmesan cheese, to serve

1 Wash the salad leaves and break into bite-sized pieces. Arrange on 4 serving plates.

2 Cut the bread into neat cubes. Heat 15 g (½ oz) butter and 2 tablespoons oil in a frying pan, add the garlic and bread cubes and fry for 2–3 minutes, stirring, until golden and crisp. Drain on kitchen paper and reserve.

3 Heat the remaining butter and oil in the frying pan and sauté the mushrooms and shallots over a moderate heat for 2–3 minutes, stirring frequently. Stir in the chives, vinegar, lemon juice, sugar and salt and pepper to taste and simmer for 30 seconds.

4 Spoon the mixture over the salad leaves and scatter with the garlic croûtons and shavings of Parmesan cheese. Serve at once.

Tapenade
Serves 6

75 g (3 oz) tinned anchovy fillets, drained

2 tablespoons milk

175 g (6 oz) pitted black olives

5 tablespoons drained capers

100-g (3½-oz) tin tuna fish in oil, drained

1 teaspoon mustard powder

150 ml (¼ pint) extra-virgin olive oil

1 tablespoon lemon juice

2 tablespoons brandy

freshly ground black pepper

selection of hot, toasted breads (such as pittas, French bread or Ciabatta), to serve

1 Soak the anchovies in the milk for 15 minutes, then drain.

2 Place the anchovies, olives, capers, tuna and mustard in a blender or food processor and blend to a smooth paste.

3 Turn the mixture into a bowl and stir in the oil and lemon juice, drop by drop (as if making mayonnaise).

4 Finally, stir in the brandy and freshly ground pepper to taste. Transfer the mixture to a serving dish. Serve with a selection of hot, toasted breads.

Mixed Seafood with Lemony Garlic Sauce
Serves 4

4 tablespoons extra-virgin olive oil *or* olive oil

2 garlic cloves, crushed

1 onion, finely chopped

2 thin-skinned lemons, sliced

2 tablespoons sweet chilli sauce

2 tablespoons soft brown sugar

900 g (2 lb) cooked, mixed seafood (peeled prawns, squid rings, mussels)

salt and freshly ground black pepper

warm, crusty bread, to serve

1 Heat the oil in a large frying pan, add the garlic and onion and cook very gently to soften. Add the lemon slices and cook gently for 2 minutes, turning them halfway through cooking.

2 Stir in the chilli sauce and sugar and remove the pan from the heat. Leave to cool.

3 Place the mixed seafood in a serving dish, pour over the cooled sauce and mix together lightly. Season with salt and pepper to taste.

4 Chill for at least 2 hours before serving with warm, crusty bread.

Little Roquefort Quiches

Serves 6

For the pastry

225 g (8 oz) plain flour

pinch of salt

1 egg, beaten

4 tablespoons olive oil

3 tablespoons water

For the filling

2 tablespoons olive oil

1 bunch spring onions, trimmed and chopped

1 garlic clove, crushed

3 eggs

200 ml (7 fl oz) single cream

salt and freshly ground black pepper

100 g (4 oz) Roquefort cheese, crumbled

1 To make the pastry, sift the flour and salt into a bowl and make a well in the centre. Add the egg, oil and water to the well and mix quickly with a fork to form a dough. Knead gently on a floured surface, then return to the bowl, cover with a damp cloth and leave to stand for 30 minutes. Pre-heat the oven to 200°C (400°F) Gas mark 6.

2 Divide the dough into six equal pieces and roll out each piece on a lightly floured surface to a round large enough to line six 11–13-cm (4½–5-in) diameter, 2-cm (¾-in) deep, loose-bottomed fluted flan tins. Trim the top edges and prick the bases several times with a fork.

3 Line the tins with foil and baking beans and cook in the oven for 5 minutes, then remove the foil and beans and cook for a further 6–8 minutes until the pastry is golden brown. Remove from the oven and reduce temperature to 180°C (350°F) Gas mark 4.

4 Next, prepare the filling. Heat the oil in a frying pan, add the spring onions and garlic and cook gently for 3 minutes. Leave to cool slightly.

5 Beat the eggs with the cream and season with salt and pepper to taste. Spoon the onion mixture and the crumbled cheese evenly into the prepared pastry cases and pour the egg mixture over.

6 Cook in the oven for about 15 minutes until the filling has set and is lightly golden. Serve warm or cold.

Roasted Mixed Peppers with Avocado and Olive Crème Fraîche

Serves 6

2 red peppers

2 orange peppers

2 yellow peppers

2 ripe avocados

3 shallots, thinly sliced

6 tablespoons extra-virgin olive oil

1 garlic clove, crushed

finely grated rind and juice of 1 lemon

salt and freshly ground black pepper

300 ml (½ pint) crème fraîche

50 g (2 oz) pitted black *or* green olives, cut into slivers

1–2 tablespoons chopped fresh oregano *or* marjoram

oregano *or* marjoram leaves, for sprinkling

warm, crusty bread, to serve

1 Place the peppers under a hot grill until the skins blister and blacken. Place peppers in a polythene bag and leave until cool enough to handle.

2 Carefully peel off the skins, discarding stalk ends and seeds, and cut the peppers into chunky strips. Place the pepper strips in a shallow dish.

3 Halve, stone and peel the avocados, slice the flesh and arrange with the peppers. Sprinkle with the shallots.

4 Whisk together the oil with the garlic, lemon rind and juice and salt and pepper to taste, and pour over the peppers, avocados and shallots. Cover and leave to marinate for at least 1 hour.

5 Mix the crème fraîche with the slivered olives and chopped oregano or marjoram. Chill.

6 Sprinkle the peppers and avocado with the oregano or marjoram leaves and serve with the crème fraîche dressing and warm, crusty bread.

Filo-wrapped Camembert with Watercress

Serves 6-8

4 tablespoons olive oil

4 spring onions, trimmed and chopped

1 small garlic clove, crushed

1 bunch watercress, trimmed and leaves coarsely chopped

50 g (2 oz) fresh white breadcrumbs

salt and freshly ground black pepper

2 tablespoons beaten egg

9 sheets of filo pastry

1 x 250-g (9-oz) whole Camembert cheese

watercress leaves and a platter of fresh fruits (such as grapes, figs, apricots, sliced pears and peaches), to serve

1 Heat 2 tablespoons olive oil in a saucepan, add the onions, garlic and watercress and cook for about 5 minutes. Stir in the breadcrumbs and salt and pepper to taste. Leave to cool slightly, then stir in 1 tablespoon of the beaten egg and mix well. Leave to cool completely.

2 Pre-heat the oven to 190°C (375°F) Gas mark 5. While working with the sheets of filo pastry, keep them covered with a damp cloth to prevent them drying out. Lay one sheet of filo pastry on a baking sheet and brush with a little oil. Diagonally cover with another sheet so that the corners just overlap the first sheet. Brush with a little oil. Repeat this process with 6 of the remaining pastry sheets, brushing each with oil before adding the next, to form a round star shape.

3 Cover the whole cheese with half the watercress mixture and place, watercress-side down, in the centre of the pastry. Press the remaining watercress mixture on top of the cheese.

4 Now bring the pastry sheets up and over the cheese to enclose it completely, folding and tucking the pastry around and over the cheese and pinching the sheets together to form a purse shape. Cut off the excess pastry from the top and press the edges flat on to the cheese to give a good shape. Now turn the pastry-wrapped cheese over and place it, join-side down, on a baking sheet.

5 Tear the remaining sheet of filo pastry into about 8 pieces. Brush the surface of the pastry-wrapped cheese with beaten egg. Crimp and pinch each of the smaller pieces of filo pastry and place on top of the cheese to

give a fluted, decorative surface.

6 Bake in the pre-heated oven for 20 minutes until golden brown. Cover with foil and cook for a further 10 minutes.

7 Remove from the oven and leave to cool for 5 minutes before serving. Place the cheese on a bed of watercress leaves and serve with a selection of fresh fruits.

Grilled Goats' Cheese on Bruschetta

Serves 4

1 large beefsteak tomato

2 garlic cloves, 1 crushed

5 tablespoons extra-virgin olive oil

1 teaspoon sugar

salt and freshly ground black pepper

2 tablespoons shredded basil leaves

8 x 2.5-cm (1-in) thick slices of Ciabatta

225 g (8 oz) chèvre (goats' cheese), thinly sliced

1 Cut the tomato into 8 thin slices and place in a dish.

2 Mix the crushed garlic clove with 4 tablespoons of oil, the sugar and salt and pepper to taste and pour over the tomatoes. Sprinkle with 1 tablespoon basil and leave to marinate for 30 minutes.

3 Lightly toast the bread slices on both sides. Cut the remaining garlic clove in half and use to rub all over both sides of toast.

4 Arrange the sliced tomatoes (reserving the marinade) over the toast and cover with the slices of cheese.

5 Grill for 2–3 minutes or until the cheese is lightly golden and melted. Drizzle with the remaining oil and sprinkle with the remaining basil. Serve warm.

Two Dips with Crudités

Serves 8-10

For the hummus

175 g (6 oz) dried chickpeas, soaked overnight in cold water

5 tablespoons lemon juice

6 tablespoons extra-virgin olive oil

3 garlic cloves, crushed

4 tablespoons tahini (sesame cream)

6 tablespoons water

salt and freshly ground black pepper

pinch of ground cumin

pinch of cayenne pepper

black olives, to garnish

For the taramasalata

100 g (4 oz) smoked cod's roe

4 slices white bread, crusts removed

a little water, for soaking

1 small onion, grated

2 garlic cloves, crushed

175 ml (6 fl oz) extra-virgin olive oil

juice of 1–2 lemons

freshly ground black pepper

lemon wedges, to garnish

a selection of raw vegetables, to serve (radishes, spring onions, mushrooms, cauliflower and broccoli florets, strips of red, green and yellow peppers, and a selection of carrot, celery and courgette sticks)

1 To make the hummus, drain the chickpeas and rinse well, then place in a saucepan. Cover with twice their volume of cold water and bring to the boil. Reduce the heat and simmer gently for about 1½–2 hours or until very soft. Drain well.

2 Put the chickpeas in a blender or food processor with the lemon juice, 4 tablespoons olive oil, garlic, tahini and water and blend to a smooth, thick and creamy purée.

3 Season with salt and pepper to taste and add the cumin and cayenne. Mix well and thin the consistency further, if wished, with more lemon juice.

4 Turn the mixture into a serving dish, cover and chill.

5 To make the taramasalata, peel the skin from the cod's roe and place in a blender or food processor. Soak the bread in a little water and squeeze out the excess. Add the bread to the blender with the onion and garlic.

6 With the machine running, very gradually add the oil and lemon juice, alternately, and a little at a time, until the mixture forms a creamy purée.

7 Season with pepper to taste and turn the mixture into a serving bowl. Cover and chill lightly.

8 Just before serving, arrange the raw vegetables on a serving platter with the two bowls of dip. Drizzle the remaining 1 tablespoon olive oil over the hummus and garnish with black olives, and garnish the taramasalata with lemon wedges.

Spanakhopitas

Serves 15

This Greek cheese and spinach pie makes an ideal light lunch or supper dish and is also perfect fare for a party.

6 tablespoons extra-virgin olive oil, plus extra for greasing

1 large onion, finely chopped

2 garlic cloves, crushed

450 g (1 lb) frozen chopped spinach, defrosted and squeezed dry

175 g (6 oz) feta cheese, crumbled

50 g (2 oz) curd cheese

1 egg, beaten

freshly ground black pepper

400 g (14 oz) filo pastry

1 Heat 2 tablespoons olive oil in a saucepan, add the onion and garlic and fry gently for 5 minutes or until softened.

2 Remove from the heat and stir in the spinach, cheeses and egg. Season with pepper to taste and mix well. Pre-heat the oven to 190°C (375°F) Gas mark 5.

3 Grease a 30 x 23-cm (12 x 9-in) baking dish with a little olive oil. Place one sheet of filo pastry in the dish, pressing the short edges up the sides of the dish at either end. Brush the pastry lightly with oil and continue layering the pastry in this way until half the pastry sheets have been added (remembering to brush each sheet with oil before adding the next).

4 Spread the spinach mixture over the pastry in the dish, then cover with the remaining sheets of pastry, brushing each one with oil before adding the next.

5 Trim the pastry at either end to neaten. Brush the surface of the pie with oil. Using a sharp knife, cut completely through all the layers to the base to make 15 portions.

6 Bake in the pre-heated oven for 30 minutes. Leave to cool for 15 minutes, then cut the portions and serve warm.

Seafood Terrine with Marinated Prawns

Serves 6-8

For the terrine

450 g (1 lb) white fish fillets, skinned, boned and cut up to make 350 g (12 oz) skinned and boned weight (use lemon sole, halibut *or* monkfish)

2 egg whites

150 ml (¼ pint) crème fraîche

2 shallots

3 tablespoons lemon juice

1 tablespoon chopped fresh tarragon

1 tablespoon chopped fresh parsley

salt and freshly ground black pepper

225 g (8 oz) mixed white and dark crabmeat

2 pinches of cayenne pepper

olive oil, for greasing

For the marinated prawns

350 g (12 oz) cooked, peeled tiger prawns *or* small, peeled prawns, if preferred

100 ml (3½ fl oz) olive oil

finely grated rind and juice of ½ lemon

1 tablespoon chopped fresh tarragon *or* parsley

1 small garlic clove, crushed

2 shallots, finely chopped

salt and freshly ground black pepper

thin slices of peeled cucumber and sprigs of tarragon, to garnish

1 Pre-heat the oven to 180°C (350°F) Gas mark 4.

2 In a blender or food processor, finely chop the fish, then add the egg whites, crème fraîche, shallots, 2 tablespoons lemon juice, tarragon, parsley and salt and pepper to taste and process to form a smooth purée.

3 In a bowl, mix the crabmeat with the cayenne and the remaining lemon juice.

4 Lightly grease a 1.2-litre (2-pint) loaf tin with olive oil and line the base with greased greaseproof paper.

5 Spoon in half the white fish mixture and level the surface. Cover with the crabmeat and top with the remaining white fish mixture, then level the surface. Cover with a sheet of oiled kitchen foil.

6 Place the loaf tin in a baking tin and add enough hot water to the baking tin to come halfway up the sides of the tin. Bake in the pre-heated oven for 40–45 minutes or until the mixture feels firm to the touch and a skewer inserted in the centre comes out clean.

7 Leave to cool in the tin, then chill for several hours.

8 Meanwhile, place the prawns in a shallow dish. Mix the oil with the lemon rind and juice, herbs, garlic, shallots and seasoning to taste. Pour over the prawns, cover and leave to marinate in the fridge for at least 2 hours, turning occasionally.

9 To serve, turn the terrine out on to a serving platter and surround with the marinated prawn mixture. Garnish the top of the terrine with rows of thin, overlapping slices of cucumber and sprigs of tarragon.

Brandade de Morue
Serves 4-6

Serve this delicious creamed salt cod dish with crisp, fried bread and a fresh green salad. Dried salt cod, a Mediterranean delicacy, is also known as bacalao. Look for fleshy, thick fillets with creamy white flesh. It is essential to soak the fish in cold water for at least 24 hours before using it in a recipe, and to change the water frequently during this time.

For the Brandade

750 g (1½ lb) salt cod

300 ml (½ pint) olive oil
(extra-virgin, if wished)

2–3 garlic cloves, crushed

250 ml (8 fl oz) single cream,
warmed

juice of ½ a lemon

freshly grated nutmeg, to taste

freshly ground black pepper

For the fried bread

about 4 tablespoons olive oil

12 slices French bread

chopped fresh parsley, to
garnish

1 Soak the fish for at least 24 hours in enough cold water to cover, changing the water frequently.

2 Drain the fish and place in a pan. Cover with fresh cold water, bring to the boil, then reduce the heat and simmer very gently for 10 minutes.

3 Drain the fish, allow to cool slightly, then remove the skin and bones and flake the flesh finely.

4 Heat 3 tablespoons olive oil in a saucepan, add the garlic, then reduce the heat to very low. Add the fish and mash the ingredients together with a wooden spoon.

5 Gradually add the remaining oil and the warmed cream, adding about 2 tablespoons of each ingredient at a time, and continue mashing the mixture together. (Take care not to let the mixture get too hot – it must not be allowed to simmer or boil.)

6 Once all the oil and cream have been added and the mixture is the consistency of creamy mashed potatoes, stir in the lemon juice, nutmeg and pepper to taste (you do not need salt).

7 Remove the pan from the heat and turn the mixture into a serving dish, set on a serving platter.

8 To make the fried bread, heat the oil in a large frying pan, add the slices of bread and fry for 2–3 minutes, turning occasionally until golden brown all over.

9 Arrange the fried bread around the dish of brandade and sprinkle with chopped parsley. Serve warm (not hot).

Soups

Avocado Soup with Prawn Salsa

Serves 4

For the soup

2 tablespoons olive oil

1 bunch spring onions, trimmed and sliced

1 tablespoon plain flour

450 ml (¾ pint) chicken stock

2 large, ripe avocados

450 ml (¾ pint) creamy milk

150 ml (¼ pint) crème fraîche

2 teaspoons lemon juice

salt and freshly ground pepper

For the prawn salsa

175 g (6 oz) peeled prawns, coarsely chopped, if wished

4 tablespoons olive oil

1 tablespoon white wine vinegar

1 tablespoon chopped fresh chives

½–1 fresh green chilli, de-seeded and finely chopped, to taste

2 spring onions, finely chopped

salt and freshly ground black pepper

1 Heat the oil in a saucepan, add the spring onions and fry gently for 2 minutes. Stir in the flour and cook for 1 minute, then stir in the stock, cover and simmer gently for 10 minutes. Leave to cool.

2 Halve the avocados, peel and remove the stones. Cut up the flesh and place in a blender or food processor with the spring onion mixture and process until smooth.

3 Add the milk, crème fraîche and lemon juice, season with salt and pepper to taste and blend until well combined. Chill for at least 2 hours before serving.

4 Meanwhile, prepare the prawn salsa. Place the prawns in a bowl. Whisk together the oil, vinegar, chives, chilli and spring onions and season with salt and pepper to taste. Pour the mixture over the prawns, cover and leave to marinate for at least 1 hour.

5 To serve, ladle the chilled soup into bowls and spoon a little of the prawn mixture into each one.

La Bourride

Serves 6

½ quantity Aïoli (see page 114)

For the stock

350 g (12 oz) fish bones, heads, tails, etc. (use only white, not oily, fish trimmings)

1 leek, sliced

1 carrot, sliced

1 celery stick, sliced

150 ml (¼ pint) dry white wine

1.2 litres (2 pints) cold water

1 small bay leaf

For the soup

4 tablespoons extra-virgin olive oil

2 leeks, cut into 1-cm (½-in) thick slices

1 onion, coarsely chopped

450 g (1 lb) potatoes, peeled, halved and cut into 5-mm (¼-in) thick slices

1.5 kg (3 lb) mixed white fish, filleted, skinned and cut into bite-sized pieces

salt and freshly ground black pepper

For the garlic bread

3–4 tablespoons extra-virgin olive oil

1 garlic clove, halved

1 French stick, cut into 12 x 1-cm (½-in) thick slices

chopped fresh parsley, to garnish

1 First make the Aïoli. Next, prepare the stock. Place the fish bones, heads and tails in a saucepan with the prepared vegetables, wine, water and bay leaf. Cover and simmer gently for 15 minutes. Strain and reserve the stock.

2 Now, prepare the fish soup. Heat the oil in a large saucepan, add the leeks, onion and potatoes and fry very gently for 10 minutes, turning occasionally.

3 Arrange the prepared fish (as well as some large, raw prawns, if desired) on top of the vegetables, pour the stock over, season with salt and pepper to taste, then cover and cook gently for 12–15 minutes or until the fish and potatoes are tender and cooked.

4 Using a draining spoon, transfer the pieces of fish and vegetables to a heated platter and keep warm.

5 Boil the stock vigorously for about 6 minutes, or until it is reduced by about a third. Leave to cool slightly, then add slowly to the prepared Aïoli, whisking vigorously all the time.

6 Return the fish mixture to the saucepan, taste and adjust the seasoning and reheat very gently, but do not allow to boil.

7 Meanwhile, prepare the garlic bread. Heat the olive oil in a frying pan, add the halved garlic clove and the slices of bread and fry until lightly golden on both sides.

8 Place two slices of fried bread in each of 6 individual soup bowls and ladle the fish soup on top. Sprinkle liberally with parsley and serve at once.

Leek and Fennel Soup with Toast and Cheese

Serves 6

6 tablespoons olive oil

1 large onion, coarsely chopped

2 leeks, trimmed, halved and thinly sliced

2 fennel bulbs, trimmed (reserving the fronds, to garnish) and coarsely chopped

1 garlic clove, crushed

3 tablespoons plain flour

1.2 litres (2 pints) rich chicken stock

salt and freshly ground black pepper

1 teaspoon lemon juice

6 x 1-cm (½-in) thick slices Ciabatta or French bread

100 g (4 oz) Gruyère *or* Emmental cheese, grated

1 Heat the oil in a saucepan, add the onion, leeks, fennel and garlic, stir well, cover and cook very gently for 15 minutes, stirring occasionally.

2 Mix in the flour and cook for 1 minute, stirring. Add the stock, salt and pepper to taste and bring to the boil, then cover and simmer gently for 20 minutes, or until the vegetables are tender.

3 Cool slightly, then purée the soup in a blender or food processor until smooth. Stir in the lemon juice and adjust the seasoning, if necessary. Reheat the soup in a clean pan.

4 Lightly toast the slices of bread on both sides. Place a slice in each of 6 flameproof soup bowls. Ladle the hot soup over the toast and sprinkle liberally with the cheese.

5 Place the bowls under a hot grill until the cheese has melted and is bubbling. Serve at once, garnished with the reserved fennel fronds.

Spiced Carrot, Lentil and Coriander Soup

Serves 6

5 tablespoons olive oil

1 large onion, sliced

450 g (1 lb) carrots, sliced

225 g (8 oz) dried red lentils

2 teaspoons ground coriander

2 teaspoons ground cumin

1.5 litres (2½ pints) chicken *or* vegetable stock

150 ml (¼ pint) single cream

300 ml (½ pint) milk

salt and freshly ground black pepper

crisp, crumbled bacon, to serve (optional)

small sprigs of coriander, to garnish

1 Heat the oil in a saucepan, add the onion and carrots, and cook gently for 5 minutes. Add the lentils, coriander and cumin, and cook for 1 minute, stirring.

2 Stir in the stock and bring to the boil. Reduce the heat, cover and simmer for about 30 minutes, or until all the ingredients are tender.

3 Leave the mixture to cool slightly, then purée in a blender or food processor. Return the soup to the pan and stir in the cream and milk and season well with salt and pepper to taste.

4 Serve hot in bowls with a scattering of crisp, crumbled bacon, if using, and garnish with small sprigs of coriander.

Creamy Garlic and Chestnut Soup

Serves 4

3 tablespoons olive oil

4 garlic cloves

1 leek, sliced

1 small onion, sliced

1.2 litres (2 pints) chicken *or* vegetable stock

2 x 240-g (8-oz) tins peeled chestnuts

150 ml (¼ pint) single cream

pinch of freshly grated nutmeg

salt and freshly ground pepper

chopped fresh chives and cream, to garnish

1 Heat the oil in a saucepan, add the garlic, leek and onion and cook very gently for 5 minutes.

2 Add the stock and chestnuts, then cover and simmer gently for 15 minutes.

3 Leave the mixture to cool slightly, then purée in a blender or food processor.

4 Return the soup to the pan and add the cream, nutmeg and salt and pepper to taste. Reheat and serve sprinkled with chopped chives and swirls of cream.

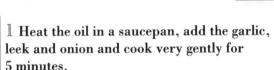

Italian Vegetable Soup

Serves 6

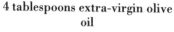

4 tablespoons extra-virgin olive
oil

6 rashers smoked streaky bacon
or pancetta, rinds removed and
chopped

1 large onion, chopped

1 leek, trimmed, halved and
thinly sliced

2 carrots, diced

2 celery sticks, sliced

2 garlic cloves, crushed

1 potato, diced

400-g (14-oz) tin chopped
tomatoes

¼ small green cabbage, finely
shredded

1.5 litres (2½ pints) chicken
stock

1 teaspoon dried oregano *or*
mixed herbs

salt and freshly ground black
pepper

300-g (11-oz) tin red kidney *or*
cannellini beans, drained and
rinsed

2 tablespoons freshly grated
Parmesan cheese

flakes of fresh Parmesan cheese,
to serve

1 Heat the oil in a saucepan, add the bacon, onion, leek, carrots, celery, garlic and potato, and fry gently for 5 minutes, stirring occasionally.

2 Stir in the tomatoes, cabbage, stock, herbs and salt and pepper to taste. Bring to the boil, then reduce the heat, cover and simmer for 20–25 minutes, or until the vegetables are tender.

3 Stir in the beans and cook for a further 5 minutes. Stir in the grated Parmesan cheese, then taste and adjust the seasoning, if necessary.

4 Serve hot, liberally sprinkled with flakes of Parmesan.

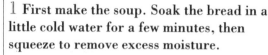

Gazpacho
Serves 6-8

For the soup

1-cm (½-in) thick slice of white bread, crusts removed

a little cold water, for soaking

1 red onion, chopped

1 garlic clove, chopped

½ cucumber, peeled and chopped

2 red peppers, de-seeded and cut up

400-g (14-oz) tin tomatoes

3 ripe tomatoes, skinned and chopped

4 tablespoons extra-virgin olive oil

900 ml (1½ pints) rich chicken stock (from a carton)

1–2 teaspoons sugar, to taste

2–3 tablespoons wine vinegar, to taste

salt and freshly ground black pepper

small bowls of diced cucumber, red onion and green pepper, to serve

For the garlic croûtons

4 tablespoons extra-virgin olive oil

1 garlic clove, crushed

3 slices of white bread, crusts removed and cut into 5-mm (¼-in) cubes

2 tablespoons chopped fresh parsley

1 First make the soup. Soak the bread in a little cold water for a few minutes, then squeeze to remove excess moisture.

2 In a bowl, mix together the onion, garlic, cucumber, red peppers, tinned and fresh tomatoes. Stir in the oil and the soaked bread.

3 Blend these ingredients together in a blender or food processor, half of the quantity at a time, until you have a coarse-textured purée.

4 Pour the mixture into a bowl and stir in the stock, sugar, vinegar and salt and pepper to taste. Chill for several hours before serving.

5 Meanwhile, prepare the garlic croûtons. Heat the oil in a frying pan, add the crushed garlic and diced bread and cook until golden brown, stirring frequently. Drain on kitchen paper and sprinkle with salt and pepper to taste and the chopped parsley.

6 Serve the chilled soup with the croûtons and bowls of diced cucumber, red onion and green pepper. Guests help themselves to the accompaniments, sprinkling them over individual servings of the soup.

Portuguese Mussel Soup

Serves 4

1.5 kg (3 lb) mussels

3 tablespoons olive oil

2 rashers smoked streaky bacon, rinds removed and chopped

4 shallots, finely chopped

2 leeks, trimmed, halved and finely shredded

1 celery stick, very thinly sliced

600 ml (1 pint) water

150 ml (¼ pint) dry white wine

3 pinches saffron strands, crushed

finely grated rind of 1 Seville orange

300 ml (½ pint) single cream

salt and freshly ground black pepper

2 tablespoons chopped fresh parsley

crusty bread, to serve

1 Discard any cracked mussels and any that remain open when tapped on the shell. Scrub the mussels, pull off the beards and soak the mussels in cold water for up to 2 hours.

2 Heat the oil in a saucepan, add the bacon, shallots, leeks and celery and cook very gently for 10 minutes.

3 Stir in 450 ml (¾ pint) water, bring to the boil, then cover and simmer gently for 25 minutes, stirring occasionally.

4 Shortly before serving, drain the mussels into another large saucepan and add the remaining water and the wine. Cover, bring to the boil and cook for 3–4 minutes, or until the mussels have opened, shaking the pan frequently to ensure that the mussels cook evenly (any mussels that remain closed should be discarded).

5 Using a draining spoon, lift the mussels out of the pan and keep warm in a large bowl, covered with a cloth.

6 Strain the liquor (in which the mussels were cooked) into the leek soup. Add the saffron, orange rind and cream, mix well and heat through, then season with salt and pepper to taste.

7 To serve, ladle the soup into large, warm soup bowls. Add the mussels and a sprinkling of parsley. Serve at once with plenty of crusty bread.

Roasted Tomato and Garlic Soup with Parmesan
Serves 4

900 g (2 lb) ripe tomatoes

7 tablespoons extra-virgin olive oil

1 whole head of garlic, just broken into cloves

1 large onion, thinly sliced

1 large carrot, thinly sliced

2 celery sticks, thinly sliced

600 ml (1 pint) good chicken stock

2 tablespoons tomato purée

1 teaspoon sugar

salt and freshly ground black pepper

flakes of fresh Parmesan and shredded basil leaves, to garnish

Ciabatta, to serve

1 Pre-heat the oven to 190°C (375°F) Gas mark 5. Halve the tomatoes and place, cut sides up, in a roasting tin. Drizzle with 2 tablespoons oil and roast in the oven for about 50 minutes, or until slightly blackened around the edges.

2 Meanwhile, place the garlic cloves in a separate small dish and drizzle with 1 tablespoon oil. Bake in the oven (at the same time as the tomatoes) for 15 minutes, or until very soft. Remove from the oven and leave to cool slightly, then push the soft cloves out of their skins and reserve.

3 Heat the remaining oil in a saucepan and gently cook the onion, carrot and celery for about 12 minutes, stirring occasionally.

4 Add the garlic cloves and the roasted tomatoes and their juice, the stock, tomato purée, sugar and salt and pepper to taste. Cover and simmer gently for 30 minutes.

5 Leave to cool slightly, then purée (in batches) and sieve to remove seeds and skin.

6 Reheat until piping hot and serve scattered with flakes of Parmesan and shredded basil, and chunks of Ciabatta.

Ribollita

Serves 6-8

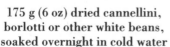

This red cabbage and bean soup is just one version of the Tuscan speciality – it is very thick and delicious.

175 g (6 oz) dried cannellini, borlotti or other white beans, soaked overnight in cold water

6 tablespoons olive oil

2 red onions, chopped

2 garlic cloves, crushed

1 celery stick, chopped

1 leek, trimmed, halved and sliced

450 g (1 lb) red cabbage, cored and coarsely shredded

100 g (4 oz) pancetta *or* smoked streaky bacon rashers, rinds removed and chopped

1 tablespoon red wine vinegar *or* balsamic vinegar

1.75 litres (3 pints) beef stock

400-g (14-oz) tin chopped tomatoes

2 tablespoons coarsely chopped fresh parsley

salt and freshly ground black pepper

For the garnish

2 garlic cloves, crushed

5 tablespoons olive oil

½ teaspoon finely chopped fresh rosemary *or* oregano

6–8 slices Ciabatta, toasted

50 g (2 oz) freshly grated Parmesan cheese

1 Drain the beans and put into a saucepan. Cover with water, bring to the boil and boil vigorously for 10 minutes. Drain and reserve.

2 Heat the oil in a saucepan, add the onions, garlic, celery, leek, red cabbage and pancetta or bacon and cook very gently for 15 minutes, stirring occasionally.

3 Stir in the drained beans, vinegar, stock and tomatoes. Cover and simmer gently for 1–1½ hours or until the beans are tender.

4 Pre-heat the oven to 190°C (375°F) Gas mark 5. Add the parsley to the soup and season with salt and pepper to taste. Adjust the thickness of the soup, if wished, by adding more beef stock (note that the consistency of the soup will thicken up even more once the toasted Ciabatta is added and the mixture is baked in the oven).

5 To make the garnish, in a small pan very gently fry the garlic in the hot oil for 1 minute. Remove from the heat and stir in the rosemary or oregano.

6 Arrange the slices of toast at the bottom of an ovenproof serving dish or tureen, sprinkle with half the garlic-flavoured oil and half the Parmesan cheese and ladle the soup over the top. Drizzle with the remaining garlic-flavoured oil and Parmesan and bake in the oven for 25 minutes. Serve hot.

Broccoli and Roquefort Soup

Serves 6

350 g (12 oz) broccoli

6 tablespoons olive oil

2 leeks, trimmed, halved and thinly sliced

1 potato, thinly sliced

2 tablespoons plain flour

900 ml (1½ pints) good chicken *or* vegetable stock

salt and freshly ground black pepper

300 ml (½ pint) creamy milk

6 tablespoons single cream

75–100 g (3–4 oz) Roquefort cheese, chopped

1 tablespoon chopped fresh chives

1 Divide the broccoli into florets, then cut into even-sized pieces. Cut off the stalks, thinly slice lengthways, then cut into small pieces.

2 Heat the oil in a saucepan, add the broccoli, leeks and potato and cook gently for 5 minutes, stirring occasionally.

3 Stir in the flour and cook for 1 minute, then stir in the stock and season with salt and pepper to taste.

4 Cover and simmer gently for 20 minutes. Leave to cool slightly, then purée in a blender or food processor until smooth.

5 Return the mixture to the pan, add the milk and reheat gently. Taste and adjust the seasoning, if necessary.

6 Ladle the soup into warm bowls, add a swirl of cream to each and sprinkle with the Roquefort cheese and chives. Serve hot.

Seafood

Baked Salmon Florentine en Papillote
Serves 4

5 tablespoons olive oil

1 onion, chopped

1 garlic clove, crushed

227-g (8-oz) tin chopped
tomatoes

225 g (8 oz) frozen chopped
spinach, defrosted

salt and freshly ground black
pepper

4 salmon steaks

4 thin slices of lemon

1 tablespoon coarsely chopped
fresh parsley

1 Pre-heat the oven to 190°C (375°F) Gas
mark 5.

2 Heat 3 tablespoons oil in a saucepan, add
the onion, garlic, tomatoes and spinach and
season with salt and pepper to taste. Cook,
uncovered, until the mixture is thick and the
onion tender. Remove from the heat.

3 Heat the remaining oil in a frying pan and
fry the salmon steaks on both sides until
lightly browned. Remove from the heat.

4 Cut 4 large pieces of foil, measuring about
30 cm (12 in) square. Place a quarter of the
spinach mixture in the centre and top with a
salmon steak. Drizzle each with a little of the
oily juices from the pan, then place a slice of
lemon and a sprinkling of parsley on top.
Season with salt and pepper.

5 Draw up the corners of the foil and fold and
pinch well together to seal, completely
enclosing the filling. Place in a baking tin and
cook in the pre-heated oven for about
15 minutes, or until the salmon is cooked and
flakes easily. Serve hot.

Crab Cakes with Tomato Salsa
Makes 8

For the crab cakes
450 g (1 lb) white and dark crabmeat

1 tablespoon olive oil

6 spring onions, finely chopped

1 tablespoon tomato ketchup

2 tablespoons mayonnaise

finely grated rind of ½ a lemon

1 tablespoon lemon juice

1 tablespoon chopped fresh parsley

100 g (4 oz) fresh white breadcrumbs

1 egg, beaten

2 tablespoons capers, drained and chopped

salt and freshly ground black pepper

For the Tomato Salsa
6 tablespoons olive oil

2 garlic cloves, crushed

4 large tomatoes, finely chopped

1½ tablespoons sweet *or* hot chilli sauce

1 tablespoon sugar

4 tablespoons lemon juice

For the coating
1 egg, beaten

75 g (3 oz) fresh white breadcrumbs

olive oil, for frying

1 Place the crabmeat in a bowl and flake finely. Heat the oil in a saucepan, add the spring onions and cook gently for 3 minutes, stirring. Remove from the heat and add to the crabmeat.

2 Stir in the tomato ketchup, mayonnaise, lemon rind and juice, parsley, breadcrumbs, beaten egg, capers and salt and pepper to taste. Mix well together.

3 Form the mixture into 8 round cakes and chill for 30 minutes.

4 Meanwhile, make the Tomato Salsa. Heat the oil in a frying pan, add the garlic and tomatoes and fry gently for 5 minutes. Remove from the heat and stir in the chilli sauce, sugar, lemon juice and salt and pepper to taste; mix well.

5 To coat the crab cakes, first dip the cakes in the beaten egg and then coat in the breadcrumbs, pressing the crumbs on firmly.

6 Heat a little oil in a large frying pan and fry the crab cakes for 4–5 minutes, turning frequently until cooked through and golden brown all over. Drain on kitchen paper and serve hot with the Tomato Salsa for dipping.

Seafood in a Filo Tart

Serves 6

For the pastry case

3 tablespoons olive oil

100 g (4 oz) filo pastry sheets

For the filling

25 g (1 oz) butter

25 g (1 oz) plain flour

5 tablespoons milk

3 tablespoons crème fraîche *or* double cream

2 eggs, separated

1 tablespoon chopped fresh dill

75 g (3 oz) Emmental *or* Gruyère cheese, grated

salt and freshly ground black pepper

225 g (8 oz) ready-to-eat, cooked mixed seafood (such as mussels, squid, prawns, cockles)

sprigs of dill, to garnish

1 Grease the base and sides of a 3-cm (1–¼-in) deep, 20-cm (8-in) diameter, loose-bottomed flan tin (or use a flan ring set on a baking sheet).

2 Lay the filo pastry sheets flat and cover with a damp cloth. Using one sheet at a time, brush with oil and cover the base and sides of the tin (the sheets will overhang the edges of the tin). Cut off a little of the excess pastry, but allow the edges to stand about 2.5 cm (1 in) above the edge of the rim.

3 Once you have lined the tin with all the pastry sheets, cover it with cling film and chill for 20 minutes while preparing the filling. Pre-heat the oven to 190°C (375°F) Gas mark 5.

4 Melt the butter in a saucepan, stir in the flour and cook for 1 minute. Add the milk and crème fraîche or cream and bring to the boil, stirring. Reduce the heat and simmer for 2 minutes.

5 Remove from the heat, cool slightly and beat in the egg yolks, dill, 50 g (2 oz) cheese and season with salt and pepper to taste. Finally, mix in the seafood.

6 Whisk the egg whites until stiff and stir 2 tablespoons into the seafood mixture to soften it, then gently fold in the remainder using a metal spoon.

7 Transfer the mixture to the pastry case and sprinkle with the remaining cheese. Cook in the pre-heated oven for 25 minutes or until the filling is risen, set and golden brown (the pastry edges will become dark brown during this time, but don't worry).

8 Remove the tart from the oven and, using

scissors, trim off the dark brown edges of filo pastry, leaving about 1 cm (½ in) to form a stand-up collar. Leave to cool for 5 minutes before serving. Remove the flan tin edge and slide the pie on to a serving plate. Serve warm, garnished with sprigs of dill.

Marinated Monkfish, Salmon and Scallop Brochettes

Serves 4

450 g (1 lb) filleted monkfish

225 g (8 oz) salmon fillets, skinned and boned

12 scallops, shelled

5 tablespoons extra-virgin olive oil *or* olive oil

finely grated rind and juice of 1 lemon

3 tablespoons dry vermouth

salt and freshly ground black pepper

4 shallots, finely chopped

150 ml (¼ pint) dry white wine

150 ml (¼ pint) fish stock

1 teaspoon crushed green peppercorns

1 tablespoon chopped fresh chives

100 ml (3½ fl oz) double cream

1 red pepper, de-seeded and cut into 16 pieces

8 spring onion bulbs

lemon and lime wedges, to garnish

1 Cut the monkfish and salmon into bite-sized pieces, about the same size as the scallops. Put the fish and scallops in a shallow dish.

2. Mix 2 tablespoons oil with the lemon rind and juice, vermouth and salt and pepper to taste, and drizzle over the fish. Cover and leave to marinate in the fridge for 1 hour.

3 Meanwhile, heat 2 tablespoons oil in a frying pan. Add the shallots and cook gently for 3 minutes. Stir in the wine, fish stock and crushed peppercorns, bring to the boil and boil for 2 minutes. Remove from the heat and stir in the chives and cream.

4 Divide the marinated fish and scallops, red pepper and spring onion bulbs into 4 portions, and thread on to 4 long, oiled metal skewers or 8 small skewers; reserve the marinade. Brush the ingredients with the remaining oil.

5 Pre-heat the grill and cook the brochettes for about 10 minutes, turning and basting frequently with the marinade, until the fish is cooked through. Reheat the creamy sauce.

6 Garnish the brochettes with lemon and lime wedges and serve at once with the sauce.

Stuffed Sole with Cheese and Pesto Crust

Serves 4

4 tablespoons Parsley Pesto (see page 117)

4 large lemon sole fillets, skinned and boned

175 g (6 oz) cooked, peeled prawns

2 shallots, finely chopped

salt and freshly ground black pepper

2 tablespoons olive oil

2 tablespoons lime juice

150 ml (¼ pint) dry vermouth *or* dry white wine

40 g (1½ oz) butter

3 tablespoons plain flour

300 ml (½ pint) fish stock

4 tablespoons single cream

50 g (2 oz) soft cheese with garlic and herbs

50 g (2 oz) coarse white breadcrumbs *or* finely chopped white bread

1–2 tablespoons freshly grated Parmesan cheese

1 Pre-heat the oven to 190°C (375°F) Gas mark 5. Make the Parsley Pesto, following the recipe on page 117.

2 Divide each sole fillet along the natural line into two fillets. Place on a board and cover half of each fillet with prawns and sprinkle with shallots and salt and pepper to taste. Fold the uncovered half of each fillet over the stuffing.

3 Heat the oil in a large frying pan, add the folded fish fillets, lime juice and vermouth. Cover and poach gently for 5 minutes. Using a fish slice, transfer the fillets to a shallow, ovenproof dish. Reserve the cooking liquor.

4 Melt the butter in a saucepan, stir in the flour and cook for 1 minute. Stir in the reserved cooking liquid and the stock and bring to the boil, stirring all the time. Reduce the heat and simmer for 2 minutes. Remove from the heat and stir in the cream and soft cheese and adjust the seasoning if necessary.

5 Pour the sauce over the fish. Mix the coarse breadcrumbs or finely chopped bread with the Pesto sauce, scatter over the fish dish and sprinkle with the grated cheese.

6 Cook in the pre-heated oven for 15 minutes or until the topping is crisp and lightly golden. Serve at once.

Steamed Mussels in Tomato Sauce

Serves 4-6

1.5 kg (3 lb) mussels

4 tablespoons extra-virgin olive oil

1 large Spanish onion, chopped

2 garlic cloves, crushed

6 rashers pancetta *or* smoked streaky bacon, rinds removed and chopped

300 ml (½ pint) dry white wine

150 ml (¼ pint) water

400-g (14-oz) tin chopped tomatoes

½–1 teaspoon chopped fresh thyme, to taste

1 tablespoon sugar

salt and freshly ground black pepper

150 ml (¼ pint) double cream

warm, crusty bread, to serve

1 Discard any cracked mussels and any that remain open when tapped on the shell. Scrub the mussels, pull off the beards and soak the mussels in cold water for up to 2 hours.

2 Heat the oil in a saucepan, add the onion, garlic and pancetta or bacon and cook gently for 3 minutes. Add 150 ml (¼ pint) wine and the water, chopped tomatoes, thyme, sugar and salt and pepper to taste. Cover and simmer for 15 minutes, stirring occasionally.

3 Meanwhile, drain and rinse the mussels. Place in a large saucepan with the remaining wine. Cover the pan tightly and place over a high heat. Steam the mussels, shaking the pan frequently, for 3–5 minutes until the mussels have opened. Discard any mussels that remain closed.

4 Strain the cooking liquor into the tomato mixture and add the cream. Taste and adjust the seasoning, if necessary.

5 Ladle the tomato mixture into 4 or 6 serving bowls and top with the mussels. Serve with warm, crusty bread for mopping up the delicious juices.

Note: To eat, use an empty shell like a pair of tweezers to pinch the mussels from their shells. Set a plate beside each guest for the empty shells. You will also need to provide spoons for the tomato sauce.

Spanish-Style Sardines

Serves 4

3 tablespoons olive oil

1 large Spanish onion, halved and very thinly sliced

1 garlic clove, crushed

4 tablespoons chopped fresh parsley

3 tablespoons chopped capers

finely grated rind and juice of 1 lemon

salt and freshly ground black pepper

16 fresh sardines, scaled and gutted

1 tablespoon wine vinegar

pinch of cayenne pepper

lemon wedges, dipped in chopped parsley, to garnish

fresh, crusty bread and a green salad, to serve

1 Pre-heat the oven to 180°C (350°F) Gas mark 4.

2 Heat 2 tablespoons oil in a frying pan and gently fry the onion and garlic for 5 minutes. Transfer the mixture to a shallow, ovenproof dish.

3 Mix together the parsley, capers, lemon rind and salt and pepper to taste. Arrange the sardines over the onions and sprinkle with the parsley mixture.

4 Whisk the vinegar with the remaining oil, lemon juice and cayenne pepper and drizzle over the sardines.

5 Cover with foil and bake in the pre-heated oven for 20 minutes. Uncover and continue cooking for a further 10 minutes.

6 Garnish with lemon wedges dipped in chopped parsley and serve warm or cold with fresh, crusty bread and a green salad.

Fritto Misto di Mare

Serves 4

1 quantity Tartare Sauce (see page 114)

For the fish and seafood

4 tablespoons plain flour

salt and freshly ground black pepper

2 sole *or* plaice fillets, skinned, boned and cut into thin strips

225 g (8 oz) prepared squid

100 g (4 oz) whitebait

2 eggs, beaten

100 g (4 oz) fresh white breadcrumbs

12 large, cooked king prawns, peeled

For the batter

100 g (4 oz) plain flour

1 tablespoon olive oil

100 ml (3½ fl oz) cold water

2 egg whites

olive oil, for frying

lemon wedges, to garnish

1 First, prepare the Tartare Sauce as given on page 114.

2 Mix the flour with salt and pepper to taste in a polythene bag, add the fish strips and shake to coat evenly. Repeat this process with the squid and the whitebait.

3 Place the beaten eggs in a shallow dish and the breadcrumbs on a plate. Dip the fish and whitebait (but not the squid or prawns) into the egg and then in the breadcrumbs to coat evenly, pressing the crumbs on firmly. Keep each type of fish separate.

4 To make the batter, place the flour and a pinch of salt in a bowl and make a well in the centre. Add the oil to the well and gradually stir in the water, then beat with a wooden spoon until smooth. Whisk the egg whites until stiff and fold into the batter using a metal spoon.

5 Dip the prawns in the prepared batter to coat, then add the remaining batter to the reserved squid and coat evenly.

6 Pour olive oil into a large frying pan until it is a third full and heat to 180°C (350°F) or until a cube of day-old bread browns in 30 seconds.

7 Fry each type of fish separately, starting with the squid, then the prawns, the fish strips and finally the whitebait. Fry each type of fish for about 2 minutes until golden brown and cooked through. Drain and keep warm while cooking the remainder in the same way.

8 Arrange each fish in separate sections on a warm serving platter. Garnish with lemon wedges and serve with plenty of Tartare sauce.

Monkfish in Aubergine 'Cannelloni' with Mushroom Sauce

Serves 4

For the fish and Aubergine 'Cannelloni'

750-g (1½-lb) filleted monkfish

150 ml (¼ pint) extra-virgin olive oil *or* olive oil

salt

juice of 1 lime

1 tablespoon chopped fresh dill *or* coriander

1 teaspoon crushed mixed coloured peppercorns

2 large aubergines, trimmed

For the Mushroom Sauce

75 g (3 oz) butter

4 shallots, finely chopped

225–350 g (8–12 oz) mixed mushrooms, sliced

juice of ½ a lemon

150 ml (¼ pint) dry white wine

150 ml (¼ pint) fish *or* chicken stock

150 ml (¼ pint) double cream *or* crème fraîche

2 tablespoons chopped fresh chives

freshly ground black pepper

1 Cut the monkfish into 20 equal pieces and place in a shallow dish. Add 1 tablespoon oil, salt to taste, lime juice, dill or coriander and crushed peppercorns. Stir lightly, then cover and marinate in the fridge for at least 30 minutes.

2 Pre-heat the oven to 200°C (400°F) Gas mark 6. Cut the aubergines lengthways into 20 thin slices. Dissolve 1½ tablespoons salt in a bowl containing 1.75 litres (3 pints) hot water. Add the aubergine slices and leave to soak for 15 minutes, weighed down with a plate to keep the slices submerged in the liquid.

3 Drain the aubergine and squeeze out excess moisture by pressing each slice between your hands and pat dry with kitchen paper.

4 Brush the aubergine slices on both sides with oil and grill, turning frequently, until golden. Leave to cool, while cooking the remainder in the same way.

5 Wrap each piece of fish in a slice of aubergine to form neat rolls. Place, join sides down, in a single layer in a shallow ovenproof dish and sprinkle with salt and pepper to taste.

6 Cook, uncovered, in the oven for 12–15 minutes, or until the fish is cooked and flakes easily.

7 Meanwhile, make the Mushroom Sauce. Heat the butter in a saucepan, add the shallots and mushrooms, sprinkle with the lemon juice, then cover and cook for 5 minutes. Using a draining spoon, remove the mushrooms from the pan and reserve.

8 Add the wine and stock to the juices in the

pan and boil vigorously to reduce slightly. Whisk in the cream or crème fraîche, stir in the mushrooms and chives and heat through. Season with salt and pepper to taste and serve hot with the Monkfish in Aubergine 'Cannelloni'.

Greek-Style Lemon Fish with Potatoes

Serves 4

1.25-kg (2½-lb) whole red snapper, hake *or* bream, cleaned (or use any other whole fish of your choice)

juice of 2 lemons

salt and freshly ground black pepper

750 g (1½ lb) potatoes, peeled and thinly sliced

1 onion, finely chopped

100 ml (3½ fl oz) extra-virgin olive oil *or* olive oil

1 tablespoon chopped capers

1 tablespoon chopped fresh oregano *or* marjoram

1 Pre-heat the oven to 180°C (350°F) Gas mark 4.

2 Make 3 diagonal slashes on each side of the fish. Brush the fish all over with a little of the lemon juice and sprinkle with salt and pepper to taste.

3 Place the fish in a large, greased, shallow, ovenproof dish. Arrange the potato slices, overlapping, around the fish.

4 Sprinkle the fish and potatoes with the remaining lemon juice and scatter with the finely chopped onion. Reserve 2 tablespoons oil and spoon the remainder over the fish and potatoes. Season potatoes with salt and pepper to taste.

5 Cover with foil and cook in the pre-heated oven for 50 minutes.

6 Uncover the dish and scatter with capers and oregano or marjoram. Drizzle with the reserved oil and continue cooking for a further 10 minutes, or until the fish is cooked and the potatoes are tender and golden.

Mediterranean Seafood Gratinées

Serves 6

450-g (1-lb) halibut fillet, skinned and boned

4 tablespoons extra-virgin olive oil *or* olive oil

2 leeks, trimmed, halved and thinly shredded

300 ml (½ pint) dry white wine

300 ml (½ pint) fish stock

1 sprig of fresh thyme

225 g (8 oz) raw shelled scallops, sliced

225 g (8 oz) cooked shelled mussels

225 g (8 oz) cooked peeled prawns

For the sauce

2 tablespoons olive oil

15 g (½ oz) butter

40 g (1½ oz) plain flour

150 ml (¼ pint) double cream

finely grated rind of ½ a lemon

1 tablespoon chopped fresh parsley

salt and freshly ground black pepper

75 g (3 oz) Gruyère cheese, grated

1 Pre-heat the oven to 180°C (350°F) Gas mark 4.

2 Cut the halibut into bite-sized pieces. Heat the oil in a frying pan, add the leeks and fry gently for 5 minutes.

3 Add the halibut, wine, stock and thyme. Bring to the boil, cover and simmer for 4 minutes.

4 Discard the thyme. Using a draining spoon, remove the fish and vegetable mixture and arrange in 6 individual ramekins.

5 Add the scallops, mussels and prawns to the pan, cover and cook gently for 2 minutes. Remove from the heat and, using a draining spoon, transfer the seafood to the halibut in the ramekins (reserve the cooking liquor).

6 To make the sauce, heat the oil and butter in a saucepan, stir in the flour and cook for 1 minute. Add the reserved cooking liquor and bring to the boil, stirring, then reduce the heat and simmer for 2 minutes, stirring all the time. Add the cream, lemon rind, parsley and salt and pepper to taste. Reheat and pour over the ramekins.

7 Sprinkle with the cheese and bake in the pre-heated oven for 12–15 minutes until golden brown and heated through. Serve at once.

Salads

Bitter-Sweet Duckling Salad

Serves 4-6

For the salad

4 boneless duckling breasts

salt and freshly ground black pepper

1 tablespoon clear honey

½ head curly endive, washed and dried

1 small head radicchio, leaves separated, washed and dried

1 head of chicory, separated into leaves, washed and dried

1 orange *or* yellow pepper, de-seeded and cut into thin strips

2 small oranges

25 g (1 oz) flaked almonds, toasted

For the dressing

6 tablespoons extra-virgin olive oil *or* olive oil

2 tablespoons cider *or* sherry vinegar

1 teaspoon wholegrain mustard

1 tablespoon clear honey

½ small garlic clove, crushed (optional)

50 g (2 oz) sun-dried tomatoes in oil, drained and sliced

salt and freshly ground black pepper

1 Pre-heat the oven to 200°C (400°F) Gas mark 6. Place the duckling breasts on a rack in a roasting tin and prick the skin all over with a fork. Sprinkle with salt and pepper to taste. Bake in the pre-heated oven for 20 minutes.

2 Remove the duckling breasts from the oven and brush with the honey, then return to the oven and continue cooking for a further 10 minutes. Remove from the oven and leave to cool slightly while preparing the salad.

3 Tear the endive and radicchio into bite-sized pieces and place in a large bowl. Break the chicory leaves in half and add to the bowl together with the pepper strips.

4 Finely grate the rind of 1 of the oranges and reserve. On a plate, peel the oranges, using a sharp knife to cut away all the bitter white pith. Cut the segments of fruit from the membranes and add to the bowl of salad leaves. Squeeze the membranes to extract any juice and reserve the juice.

5 Put the dressing ingredients in a screw-topped jar and add the reserved orange rind and juice. Shake vigorously until well blended.

6 Cut the cooled (though still warm) duck breasts into thin strips and add to the salad.

7 Shake the dressing once again and pour over the salad. Toss the ingredients lightly together and serve at once, scattered with toasted almonds.

Salade Niçoise

Serves 4

For the salad

225 g (8 oz) French beans, topped and tailed, if wished

1 garlic clove, halved

1 small iceberg lettuce, leaves separated, washed and dried

2 hard-boiled eggs, shelled and cut into wedges

3 tomatoes, cut into wedges

1 green pepper, de-seeded and cut into rings

1 small onion, sliced and separated into rings

¼ cucumber, sliced

50-g (2-oz) tin anchovy fillets, drained

198-g (7-oz) tin tuna in oil *or* brine, drained and roughly flaked

12 black olives

For the dressing

150 ml (¼ pint) extra-virgin olive oil

3 tablespoons wine vinegar

1–2 tablespoons chopped fresh herbs (a mixture of chives, parsley and marjoram)

1 teaspoon Dijon mustard

½ teaspoon caster sugar

salt and freshly ground black pepper

1 Cook the French beans in a saucepan of lightly salted, boiling water for about 6 minutes until tender-crisp. Drain, refresh in cold water and drain again. Pat dry on kitchen paper and cool.

2 Rub the serving bowl with the cut garlic clove. Use the lettuce to line the bowl and arrange all the prepared ingredients on top, keeping each ingredient in a separate group.

3 Place all the dressing ingredients in a screw-topped jar and shake vigorously until well blended. Drizzle over the salad and serve at once.

Chicken and Melon Salad in Spiced Mayonnaise

Serves 6

For the salad

750 g (1½ lb) cooked chicken, cut into small, bite-sized pieces

1 small, ripe Charentais melon, de-seeded and cut into neat pieces

For the spiced Mayonnaise

1 quantity Mayonnaise (see page 114)

2 tablespoons olive oil

½ teaspoon cumin seeds

1 fresh, green chilli, de-seeded and finely chopped

1 onion, finely chopped

1 garlic clove, crushed

1–2 teaspoons sweet chilli sauce, to taste

150 ml (¼ pint) chicken stock

1 tablespoon tomato purée

juice of ½ a lemon

2 tablespoons fruit chutney, chopped if necessary

3–4 tablespoons double cream *or* crème fraîche

salt and freshly ground black pepper

25 g (1 oz) pine nuts *or* flaked almonds, toasted, to garnish

1 Place the chicken and melon pieces in a large bowl, cover and chill while preparing the spiced Mayonnaise.

2 Make the Mayonnaise, following the recipe on page 114, and reserve.

3 Heat the oil in a saucepan, add the cumin seeds, chilli, onion and garlic and cook very gently for 5 minutes, without colouring, stirring frequently.

4 Stir in the chilli sauce, stock, tomato purée, lemon juice and chutney. Cook gently for 5 minutes. Remove from the heat and leave to cool.

5 Mix the Mayonnaise with the cream or crème fraîche and the cold spiced onion mixture and season with salt and pepper to taste. Add to the chicken and melon mixture and mix lightly together.

6 Transfer the mixture to a serving platter and scatter with the toasted pine nuts or almonds.

Fruited Goats' Cheese Salad

Serves 4

This salad is also extremely good using slices of ripe Brie or Camembert instead of goats' cheese.

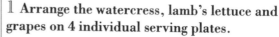

1 bunch watercress, stalks trimmed, washed and dried

handful of lamb's lettuce, washed and dried

100 g (4 oz) seedless red *or* green grapes

7 tablespoons extra-virgin olive oil

8 x 1-cm (½-in) thick slices French bread

1 garlic clove, halved

2 ripe pears, peeled, quartered and cored

2 tablespoons lemon juice

175–225 g (6–8 oz) goats' cheese, thinly sliced

a little cayenne pepper, for sprinkling

1 Arrange the watercress, lamb's lettuce and grapes on 4 individual serving plates.

2 Heat 3–4 tablespoons oil in a frying pan, add the bread slices and fry until golden brown on both sides. Drain and rub all over with the cut garlic clove.

3 Cut each pear quarter into 3 slices and brush with a little of the lemon juice. Arrange 3 pear slices on each piece of fried bread and top with the slices of goats' cheese.

4 Sprinkle each one with a pinch of cayenne and cook under a hot grill for about 2 minutes, or until the cheese has melted and is beginning to brown.

5 Meanwhile, whisk the remaining oil and lemon juice together and drizzle over the salad leaves and grapes. Arrange 2 of the pear and cheese toasts on each plate of salad and serve at once.

Pasta Salad with Hummus Sesame Dressing

Serves 4

225 g (8 oz) dried pasta shapes (such as penne, rigatoni, twists)

3 tablespoons sesame seeds

440-g (15-oz) tin chickpeas, drained

3 garlic cloves

4 tablespoons extra-virgin olive oil

juice of 1½ lemons

4 tablespoons water

½ teaspoon ground cumin

¼ teaspoon chilli powder

1 bunch spring onions, halved and sliced

1 tablespoon chopped fresh parsley

½ green pepper, de-seeded and fairly finely chopped

salt and freshly ground black pepper

6 tablespoons Mayonnaise (see page 114)

slivers of black and green olives, to garnish

1 Cook the pasta in a large saucepan of boiling, salted water for 10–12 minutes or until *al dente* (tender, but still slightly firm to the bite).

2 Meanwhile, toast the sesame seeds until lightly golden. Place the chickpeas in a blender or food processor with the garlic, oil, lemon juice, water, 2 tablespoons sesame seeds, cumin and chilli powder. Process until the mixture forms a creamy paste.

3 Turn the mixture into a large bowl. Add the spring onions, parsley and green pepper, mix well and season with salt and pepper to taste.

4 Drain the cooked pasta and, while still hot, add to the bowl of hummus dressing and turn in the mixture until well coated. Leave to cool.

5 Just before serving, mix in the Mayonnaise and turn the mixture into a serving bowl. Sprinkle with the remaining toasted sesame seeds and garnish with slivers of black and green olives.

Leafy Salad with Bacon and Brioche Croûtons

Serves 4-6

For the salad

350 g (12 oz) mixed salad leaves (such as cos lettuce, oak-leaf lettuce, rocket and young spinach)

6 shallots, sliced and separated into rings

12 cherry tomatoes, halved

8 rashers smoked streaky bacon, rinds removed and cut into strips

2 tablespoons extra-virgin olive oil

2 brioche, sliced and cubed

For the dressing

2 egg yolks

1 garlic clove, crushed

½ teaspoon Dijon mustard

4 anchovy fillets, finely mashed

2 tablespoons lemon juice

2 tablespoons freshly grated Parmesan *or* Pecorino cheese

1 teaspoon caster sugar

5 tablespoons extra-virgin olive oil

freshly ground black pepper

1 First, prepare the dressing. In a bowl, mix the egg yolks with the garlic, mustard, anchovies, lemon juice, cheese and sugar. Gradually mix in the oil, whisking well to give a smooth dressing. Season with pepper to taste.

2 Next, prepare the salad. Place the prepared salad leaves, shallots and cherry tomatoes in a serving bowl.

3 Dry-fry the bacon in a frying pan until crisp and golden. Remove from the pan and scatter over the salad.

4 Heat the oil in the same frying pan and fry the brioche cubes until golden and crisp, turning frequently.

5 Add the dressing to the salad and toss lightly until all ingredients are evenly coated. Scatter the croûtons over the salad and serve at once.

Sunshine Fruit and Avocado Salad

Serves 6

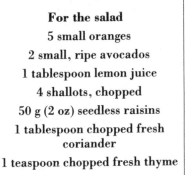

A refreshing salad to serve with cold meats and poultry or with grilled fish.

For the salad

5 small oranges

2 small, ripe avocados

1 tablespoon lemon juice

4 shallots, chopped

50 g (2 oz) seedless raisins

1 tablespoon chopped fresh coriander

1 teaspoon chopped fresh thyme

For the dressing

6 tablespoons extra-virgin olive oil

juice of 1 small orange

2 tablespoons dry sherry

1 tablespoon clear honey

salt and freshly ground black pepper

1 Using a sharp knife, peel the oranges, removing all the bitter white pith. Cut oranges into neat slices.

2 Halve, peel and stone the avocados. Cut into slices and brush with lemon juice.

3 Arrange the orange and avocado slices in layers in a serving bowl, scattering each layer with shallots, raisins and herbs.

4 To make the dressing, whisk the oil with the orange juice, sherry, honey and salt and pepper to taste. Pour the dressing over the salad, cover and leave to marinate in the fridge for at least 1 hour before serving.

Eggs Tonnato on Pepperoni

Serves 6

This dish makes a delicious starter, light lunch or supper dish. Watch out for jars of pepperoni (sliced red and yellow peppers in oil) in supermarkets and Italian delicatessens, or make your own (see page 128).

For the eggs

285-g (10½-oz) jar pepperoni, drained

6 hard-boiled eggs, shelled

50-g (2-oz) tin anchovy fillets, drained

1 tablespoon drained capers

sprigs of dill, to garnish

For the tonnato sauce:

½ quantity Mayonnaise (see page 114)

100-g (3½-oz) tin tuna in oil, drained

1 tablespoon lemon juice

1 tablespoon single cream

1 tablespoon drained capers

salt and freshly ground black pepper

1 First, prepare the tonnato sauce. Make the Mayonnaise as given on page 114, then put it into a blender or food processor with the tuna, lemon juice and cream and process until smooth. Stir in the capers and thin the consistency slightly more if necessary with a little extra cream. Season with salt and pepper to taste.

2 Place a spoonful of pepperoni to one side of each of 6 serving plates. Halve the eggs lengthways and arrange 2 halves on each plate. Spoon the tonnato sauce over the eggs to coat.

3 Halve each anchovy fillet lengthways, then roll up and place one on each egg. Sprinkle the sauce with capers and garnish the plates with sprigs of dill. Serve chilled.

Grilled Italian-Style Salad

Serves 4

1 garlic clove, crushed

6 tablespoons extra-virgin olive oil *or* olive oil

2 red onions, cut into wafer-thin slices

3 large beefsteak tomatoes, thinly sliced

175 g (6 oz) Mozzarella cheese, thinly sliced

1½ tablespoons balsamic vinegar

salt and freshly ground black pepper

2–3 tablespoons shredded basil leaves

1 Mix the garlic with the oil. Brush the slices of onion with some of the garlic and oil mixture and grill on both sides until beginning to brown.

2 Arrange the slices of onion, tomato and Mozzarella slightly overlapping in a large, shallow, flameproof dish.

3 Whisk the remaining garlic-flavoured oil with the vinegar and drizzle over the salad. Sprinkle with salt and pepper to taste.

4 Place under a hot grill for 3–4 minutes or until the cheese begins to melt.

5 Serve at once, sprinkled with the shredded basil leaves.

Toasted Walnut, Salami and Roquefort Salad

Serves 6

For the salad

100 g (4 oz) walnut pieces

350 g (12 oz) mixed salad leaves, prepared as necessary

selection of French salamis (you need 24 very thin slices in total), casings removed

175 g (6 oz) Roquefort *or* Saint Agur cheese, broken into small pieces

1–2 tablespoons chopped fresh chives

18 black olives

For the dressing

8 tablespoons extra-virgin olive oil *or* olive oil

2 tablespoons white wine vinegar

½ teaspoon caster sugar

1 garlic clove, crushed (optional)

salt and freshly ground black pepper

warm, crusty bread, to serve

1 Grill the walnut pieces until lightly golden, then leave to cool.

2 Arrange the mixed salad leaves on 6 individual serving plates.

3 Fold the salami slices in half, then in half again to form cone shapes. Arrange 4 cones among the salad leaves on each plate.

4 Scatter the cheese, walnut pieces and chives over each salad. Add 3 olives to each plate.

5 Place all the dressing ingredients in a screw-topped jar and shake vigorously until well blended and drizzle over each salad. Serve immediately with warm, crusty bread.

Chicken and Duck

Mozzarella-Glazed Chicken with Aubergine and Tomatoes

Serves 4

350 g (12 oz) aubergines, trimmed and cut in 1-cm (½-in) thick slices

salt

3 boneless chicken breasts, skinned

about 150 ml (¼ pint) extra-virgin olive oil *or* olive oil

2 garlic cloves, crushed

1 large onion, chopped

400-g (14-oz) tin chopped tomatoes

1 teaspoon sugar

salt and freshly ground black pepper

8 basil leaves, shredded

175 g (6 oz) Mozzarella cheese, sliced

15–25 g (½–1 oz) Parmesan cheese, freshly grated (optional)

1 Place the aubergine slices in a colander, sprinkle liberally with salt and leave for 30 minutes. Rinse the aubergine under cold water and pat dry on kitchen paper.

2 Pre-heat the oven to 190°C (375°F) Gas mark 5. Cut each chicken breast into about 5 thin diagonal slices.

3 Heat 2 tablespoons oil in a frying pan and fry the chicken slices for 2–3 minutes on each side to seal. Remove from the pan.

4 Heat another 1 tablespoon oil in the pan and fry the garlic and onion for 3 minutes. Stir in the tomatoes, sugar and salt and pepper to taste and cook for 5 minutes, stirring occasionally.

5 Heat half the remaining oil in a large frying pan, add half the aubergine slices and fry for about 2–3 minutes on each side until golden and softened. Remove from the pan and repeat this process with the remaining oil and aubergine slices (add more oil to the pan, if necessary).

6 Layer the aubergine slices in an ovenproof dish and top with the sliced chicken. Season well with salt and pepper, then pour the tomato mixture over the chicken and sprinkle with the shredded basil. Arrange the sliced Mozzarella on top and sprinkle with the grated Parmesan, if using.

7 Bake in the pre-heated oven for about 30 minutes, when golden and bubbling. Serve hot.

Spiced Orange Chicken with Lentils
Serves 4-6

3 tablespoons plain flour

1 teaspoon ground coriander

1 teaspoon ground cumin

½ teaspoon salt

freshly ground black pepper

½ teaspoon dried mixed herbs

8 chicken drumsticks

4 tablespoons olive oil

25 g (1 oz) butter

finely grated rind and juice of 1 orange

1 large onion, finely chopped

2 garlic cloves, crushed

225 g (8 oz) red lentils, washed

600 ml (1 pint) chicken stock

1-2 tablespoons clear honey

orange wedges and chopped parsley, to garnish

1 Place the flour, spices, salt, pepper to taste and herbs in a polythene bag and shake well to mix.

2 Place one chicken drumstick at a time into the flour mixture and shake well to coat evenly.

3 Heat 2 tablespoons oil and the butter in a large frying pan, add the drumsticks and fry for 3–4 minutes on each side to brown lightly.

4 Stir the orange rind and juice into the pan, then cover and cook gently for 20 minutes or until tender and cooked through.

5 Meanwhile, heat the remaining oil in a saucepan and fry the onion and garlic for 2–3 minutes. Stir in the lentils and chicken stock and bring to the boil.

6 Cover and simmer for 20 minutes until the lentils have absorbed all the stock and are tender, but still whole. Season with salt and pepper to taste.

7 Arrange the lentils on a warm serving dish and place the drumsticks on top. Stir the honey into the juices remaining in the frying pan, heat through and spoon over the chicken and lentils. Garnish with orange wedges and chopped parsley. Serve hot.

Wine-Braised Chicken Rolls with Herbed Stuffing

Serves 6-8

4 large, boneless chicken breasts, skinned

4–5 tablespoons extra-virgin olive oil

4 rashers pancetta *or* streaky bacon, rinds removed and finely chopped

1 onion, finely chopped

100 g (4 oz) fresh white breadcrumbs

1 tablespoon chopped fresh parsley

1 tablespoon chopped fresh tarragon

1 tablespoon chopped fresh chives

finely grated rind of ½ a lemon

salt and freshly ground black pepper

3 tablespoons beaten egg

12 shallots, peeled

6 small carrots, quartered

100 g (4 oz) button mushrooms, wiped

2 tablespoons plain flour

600 ml (1 pint) chicken stock

200 ml (7 fl oz) dry white wine

2 tablespoons tomato purée

sprigs of fresh herbs, to garnish

new potatoes and green beans, to serve

1 Pre-heat the oven to 180°C (350°F) Gas mark 4. Slice each chicken breast in half lengthways through the centre to give 8 thin breasts . Place between 2 sheets of dampened greaseproof paper and beat well with a meat mallet or rolling pan to give 8 thin escalopes.

2 Heat 2 tablespoons oil in a small saucepan and gently fry the pancetta or bacon and chopped onion for 5 minutes. Remove from the heat and stir in the breadcrumbs, herbs, lemon rind, salt and pepper to taste and beaten egg and mix well together.

3 Divide the stuffing evenly between the escalopes and spread out to within 1 cm (½ in) of the edges. Tidy uneven edges, then roll up and secure with cocktail sticks.

4 Heat 2 tablespoons oil in a large, flame-proof casserole and gently fry the chicken rolls for 5 minutes, turning occasionally until lightly browned, then remove.

5 Add the shallots, carrots and mushrooms to the casserole and fry gently for 5 minutes, adding a little extra oil, if necessary.

6 Stir the flour into the juices in the casserole and cook for 1 minute. Add the stock, wine and tomato purée and bring to the boil, stirring.

7 Return the chicken rolls to the casserole, then cover and cook in the pre-heated oven for about 1 hour, or until the chicken rolls are tender and cooked through.

8 Lift the chicken rolls out of the dish and carefully remove the cocktail sticks. Return the rolls to the casserole and garnish with fresh herbs. Serve hot with new potatoes and green beans.

Garlic Lemon Chicken

Serves 4

4 tablespoons plain flour

salt and freshly ground black pepper

8 small chicken portions

4–6 tablespoons extra-virgin olive oil

1 large onion, chopped

2 celery sticks, thinly sliced

1 red pepper, de-seeded and cut into strips

600 ml (1 pint) chicken stock

300 ml (½ pint) dry white wine

1 tablespoon chopped fresh tarragon

3 garlic cloves, crushed

finely grated rind and juice of 1 lemon

2–3 teaspoons green peppercorns, coarsely crushed

slices of lemon and sprigs of tarragon, to garnish

1 Pre-heat the oven to 190°C (375°F) Gas mark 5.

2 Mix the flour with salt and pepper to taste and use to coat the chicken portions. Reserve any remaining flour.

3 Heat 4 tablespoons oil in a flameproof casserole. Add the onion, celery and red pepper and fry gently for 5 minutes, stirring frequently. Remove from the pan, using a draining spoon.

4 Add the chicken pieces to the pan and fry over a moderate heat to brown the chicken on all sides (add a little more oil to the pan, if necessary).

5 Stir any reserved seasoned flour into the pan and mix well. Add the chicken stock, wine, tarragon, garlic, lemon rind and juice and the peppercorns and bring to the boil. Return the vegetables to the dish and mix well.

6 Cover and bake in the pre-heated oven for about 40 minutes, or until the chicken is tender and cooked through. Serve hot, garnished with slices of lemon and sprigs of tarragon.

Mediterranean Chicken Pasta with Garlic Crumbs

Serves 4

For the chicken and pasta

225 g (8 oz) dried pasta shapes (spirals, penne, rigatoni)

4 tablespoons extra-virgin olive oil

4 boneless chicken breasts, skinned and cut into bite-sized pieces

1 large onion, quartered and sliced

1 large green pepper, de-seeded and cut into 1-cm (½-in) pieces

100 g (4 oz) mushrooms, sliced

400-g (14-oz) tin chopped tomatoes

300 ml (½ pint) chicken stock

2 tablespoons tomato purée

½ teaspoon dried oregano

salt and freshly ground black pepper

For the sauce

40 g (1½ oz) butter

40 g (1½ oz) plain flour

450 ml (¾ pint) milk

75 g (3 oz) Cheddar cheese, grated

For the garlic crumbs

3 tablespoons olive oil

1 garlic clove, crushed

75 g (3 oz) fresh white breadcrumbs

1 Cook the pasta shapes in a saucepan of boiling, salted water for 12 minutes. Drain well and place in a large, ovenproof dish.

2 Heat the oil in a saucepan, add the chicken strips and fry, stirring, for 2–3 minutes until sealed all over. Remove from the saucepan using a draining spoon.

3 Add the onion, green pepper and mushrooms to the saucepan and fry gently for 5 minutes. Return the chicken to the saucepan and stir in the chopped tomatoes, chicken stock, tomato purée, oregano and salt and pepper to taste.

4 Cover and cook gently for 15 minutes, stirring occasionally. Meanwhile, pre-heat the oven to 190°C (375°F) Gas mark 5.

5 To make the sauce, melt the butter in a saucepan, stir in the flour and cook for 1 minute. Gradually stir in the milk and bring to the boil, stirring all the time with a wooden spoon. Reduce the heat and simmer for 2 minutes, stirring.

6 Remove from the heat and stir in half the cheese and season with salt and pepper to taste.

7 Pour the chicken mixture over the pasta in the dish and cover with the cheese sauce.

8 To make the garlic crumbs, heat the oil in a frying pan. Add the garlic and breadcrumbs and stir over a moderate heat for 2 minutes. Remove from the heat.

9 Sprinkle the breadcrumbs and the remaining cheese over the sauce. Bake in the pre-heated oven for 25–30 minutes until golden brown and bubbling. Serve hot.

Circassian-Style Chicken
Serves 6

6 boneless chicken breasts, with skin

50 g (2 oz) blanched almonds, coarsely chopped

50 g (2 oz) hazelnuts, coarsely chopped

3 tablespoons extra-virgin olive oil

150 ml (¼ pint) tomato ketchup

3 tablespoons soft brown sugar

1–2 teaspoons chilli powder

3 tablespoons wine vinegar

1 small onion, finely chopped

salt and freshly ground black pepper

300 ml (½ pint) chicken stock

1 Using a sharp knife, make 3 diagonal cuts across each chicken breast, cutting right through the skin and into the flesh each time. Place the chicken, skin side up, in a single layer in a shallow dish.

2 In a bowl, mix together the nuts, 1 tablespoon oil, tomato ketchup, sugar, chilli powder, vinegar, onion and salt and a little pepper to taste.

3 Pour over the chicken breasts, then cover and leave to marinate in the fridge for several hours, turning occasionally.

4 Lift the chicken breasts from the marinade (reserving it) and place them under a moderate grill. Drizzle with the remaining oil and cook for 15–20 minutes, turning frequently until cooked through.

5 Place the reserved marinade in a saucepan with the stock and bring to the boil, stirring. Reduce the heat and simmer gently for 5 minutes until the mixture has thickened slightly.

6 Serve the chicken breasts hot with the sauce.

Moroccan~Style Chicken in Pastry

Serves 6

100 g (4 oz) aubergine, diced

salt

3 tablespoons olive oil

1 boneless chicken breast, skinned and minced

1 garlic clove, crushed

1 onion, finely chopped

½ teaspoon ground cinnamon

1 teaspoon ground cumin

1 teaspoon ground coriander

the juice of ½ a lemon

1 tablespoon chopped fresh mint

1 egg, beaten

25 g (1 oz) fresh white *or* brown breadcrumbs

400 g (14 oz) frozen puff pastry, defrosted

beaten egg, to glaze

mixed salad and natural yogurt, to serve

1. Put the aubergine in a colander, sprinkle with salt and leave for 30 minutes. Rinse in cold water, squeeze, then pat dry with kitchen paper and chop coarsely. Pre-heat the oven to 220°C (425°F) Gas mark 7.

2 Heat the oil in a frying pan, add the chicken, garlic, onion, spices and aubergine and cook for 5 minutes, stirring occasionally. Remove from the heat and stir in the lemon juice, mint, beaten egg and breadcrumbs and season with salt to taste. Mix well and leave to cool.

3 Roll out the pastry on a lightly floured surface and trim to a 30-cm (12-in) square. Cut into two pieces, one measuring 30 x 16 cm (12 x 6½ in) and the other 30 x 14 cm (12 x 5½ in).

4 Place the smaller piece on a baking sheet and spread the cold chicken mixture over to within 1 cm (½ in) of the edges. Brush the edges with water. Lift the remaining pastry and place over the chicken mixture. Press the pastry edges together firmly to seal, then flute neatly.

5 Brush the pastry with beaten egg to glaze, then, using a sharp knife, cut diagonal slashes across the top of the pastry. Re-roll the pastry trimmings and use to make leaves for decorating the top and brush with beaten egg.

6 Bake in the pre-heated oven for 15 minutes, then reduce the oven temperature to 190°C (375°F) Gas mark 5 and continue cooking for a further 15 minutes, covering with foil during cooking, if necessary, to prevent overbrowning.

7 Serve warm or cold with a mixed salad and spoonfuls of natural yogurt.

Provençal Chicken Pepper Tart
Serves 8

For the pastry

225 g (8 oz) plain white flour

pinch of salt

1 egg, beaten

4 tablespoons olive oil

3 tablespoons water

For the filling

3 tablespoons olive oil

1 boneless chicken breast, skinned and cut into small pieces

1 red pepper, de-seeded and thinly sliced

½ yellow pepper, de-seeded and thinly sliced

1 onion, halved and thinly sliced

1 garlic clove, crushed

2 rashers streaky bacon, rinds removed and chopped

3 eggs

150 ml (¼ pint) milk

150 ml (¼ pint) double cream

salt and freshly ground black pepper

8 cherry tomatoes, halved

8 pitted black olives, halved

1 tablespoon shredded basil *or* chopped marjoram

50 g (2 oz) Gruyère cheese, grated

1 To make the pastry, place the flour and salt in a bowl and make a well in the centre. Add the egg, oil and water to the well and mix vigorously with a fork to form a dough. Knead lightly, cover with a damp cloth and leave to rest for 30 minutes.

2 Pre-heat the oven to 200°C (400°F) Gas mark 6. Roll out the pastry and use to line a 28–30-cm (11–12-in) loose-bottomed, fluted flan tin. Trim the top edge and prick the base several times with a fork. Line the case with foil, then fill with baking beans and set the flan tin on a baking sheet.

3 Cook in the pre-heated oven for 10 minutes, then remove the foil and beans and cook for a further 3 minutes. Remove from the oven and reduce the oven temperature to 190°C (375°F) Gas mark 5.

4 Heat the oil in a large frying pan, add the chicken, peppers, onion, garlic and bacon and fry gently for 5 minutes, stirring frequently. Remove from the heat and leave to cool slightly.

5 In a bowl, beat the eggs with the milk and cream and season with salt and pepper to taste. Arrange the chicken mixture in the partially cooked flan case (still in its flan tin) and add the egg mixture. Arrange the halved tomatoes and olives in the mixture, then sprinkle with the basil or marjoram and cheese.

6 Bake in the oven for about 30 minutes, or until rich golden brown and set. Serve warm or cold.

Spanish Chicken with Rice and
Serves 4
Cabanos

4 tablespoons extra-virgin olive oil

3 boneless chicken breasts, skinned and cut into thin strips

1 large onion, chopped

2 garlic cloves, crushed

350 g (12 oz) long-grain rice

2 pinches saffron strands, crushed

¼–½ teaspoon cayenne pepper, to taste

100 ml (3½ fl oz) medium-dry sherry *or* white wine

600 ml (1 pint) chicken stock

100 g (4 oz) frozen peas

2 tablespoons chopped fresh parsley

225 g (8 oz) cabanos sausage, skinned and cut into chunky slices

10 pitted black *or* green olives, cut into slivers

1 tinned pimento, quartered and slivered

salt

1 Heat the oil in a large flameproof casserole, add the chicken and fry gently until sealed all over. Stir in the onion, garlic and rice and cook for 1 minute, stirring.

2 Add the saffron, cayenne, sherry or wine and stock and bring to the boil. Cover and cook for 15 minutes.

3 Add the peas, parsley, cabanos, olives, pimento and salt to taste. Stir until just mixed, then cover and cook for a further 6–8 minutes, or until all the liquid has been absorbed and the rice is tender.

4 Fluff up with a fork and serve hot.

Glazed Duck Breasts with Apples and Calvados

Serves 6

6 x 200-g (7-oz) boned duckling breasts

a little salt

1 tablespoon clear honey

4 tablespoons olive oil

2 cooking apples, peeled, cored and cut into chunky slices

4 shallots, chopped

1 garlic clove, crushed

200 ml (⅓ pint) apple juice

300 ml (½ pint) chicken stock

4 teaspoons cornflour

5 tablespoons Calvados

½–1 teaspoon Dijon mustard, to taste

1 Pre-heat the oven to 200°C (400°F) Gas mark 6.

2. Prick the duckling skin all over and sprinkle with salt. Place, skin side up, on a rack in a roasting tin and cook in the pre-heated oven for 20 minutes.

3 Lift the duckling breasts on to a sheet of foil and place on the rack in the tin and turn up the edges slightly to retain the juices. Brush the duckling breast skin with honey and continue cooking for a further 10 minutes until the skin is crisp and golden and the flesh is cooked through.

4 Meanwhile, prepare the sauce. Heat the oil in a frying pan, add the apple slices and fry for 5 minutes, turning frequently until lightly golden. Remove from the pan and keep warm. Add the shallots and garlic to the pan and fry gently for 3 minutes.

5 Add the apple juice and stock to the pan and bring to the boil. Blend the cornflour with the Calvados and mustard, then add to the pan and simmer for 5 minutes, stirring all the time.

6 Add the duckling juices to the sauce in the pan and leave the breasts to stand for 5 minutes. Add the apple slices to the sauce and heat through.

7 Cut the duckling breasts into thin slices and arrange on serving plates, fanning them out attractively. Add several slices of apple to each plate and spoon a little of the sauce around each serving. Serve hot.

Note: This can also be made using brandy in place of Calvados.

Cassoulet of Duckling

Serves 6

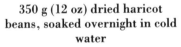

350 g (12 oz) dried haricot beans, soaked overnight in cold water

5 tablespoons extra-virgin olive oil

2 onions, halved and sliced

2 garlic cloves, crushed

3 tablespoons tomato purée

1 tablespoon chopped fresh rosemary

1 tablespoon chopped fresh thyme

3 duckling quarters, halved

225 g (8 oz) smoked bacon rashers, rinds removed and coarsely chopped

225 g (8 oz) Toulouse sausages, cut into chunky pieces

1 litre (1¾ pints) chicken stock, boiling

salt and freshly ground black pepper

50 g (2 oz) fresh white *or* brown breadcrumbs

1 Pre-heat the oven to 180°C (350°F) Gas mark 4.

2 Drain the soaked beans and put into a large saucepan with enough fresh cold water to cover. Bring to the boil and boil vigorously for 10 minutes. Drain beans and place in a large bowl.

3 Heat 3 tablespoons oil in a large, flameproof casserole, add the onions and garlic and fry gently for 5 minutes. Using a draining spoon, transfer the onions and garlic to the bowl of beans. Stir in the tomato purée and herbs and mix well.

4 Heat the remaining oil in the casserole, add the duckling portions, bacon and sausages and fry over a moderate heat until golden brown, turning frequently. Remove from the casserole.

5 Transfer half the bean mixture to the casserole dish. Top with the duck portions, bacon and sausages and cover with the remaining bean mixture.

6 Pour the stock into the casserole, then cover and cook in the pre-heated oven for 1¾ hours.

7 Remove the lid from the casserole and season the cassoulet with salt and pepper to taste. Sprinkle the surface with the breadcrumbs, return to the oven and continue cooking, uncovered, for a further 30–40 minutes, or until the topping is golden brown and crisp. Serve hot.

Meats

Wine-Braised Beef with Porcini
Serves 6

1.5 kg (3 lb) lean braising steak

6 tablespoons extra-virgin olive oil *or* olive oil

6 rashers streaky bacon, rinds removed and chopped

2 leeks, sliced

450 g (1 lb) shallots

2 garlic cloves, crushed

6 tablespoons plain flour

1.2 litres (2 pints) good beef stock

600 ml (1 pint) red wine

227-g (8-oz) tin chopped tomatoes

2 teaspoons balsamic vinegar

2 teaspoons chopped fresh thyme

salt and freshly ground black pepper

2 x 15-g (½-oz) packets dried porcini

600 ml (1 pint) warm water

397-g (14-oz) tin artichoke hearts, drained and halved

1 Pre-heat the oven to 190°C (375°F) Gas mark 5.

2 Trim the steak and cut into bite-sized pieces. Heat the oil in a large, flameproof casserole and brown the meat in batches. Using a draining spoon, transfer the meat to a plate and reserve.

3 Add the bacon, leeks, shallots and garlic to the casserole and cook for 2 minutes. Stir the flour into the casserole and cook for 1 minute. Add the stock and wine, stir well and bring to the boil, stirring.

4 Return the meat to the casserole and add the tomatoes, vinegar and thyme and season with salt and pepper to taste. Cover and bake in the pre-heated oven for 1¾ hours.

5 Meanwhile, cover the porcini with the warm water and leave to soak for 20–30 minutes. Drain, reserving the liquid. Cut the porcini into even-sized pieces.

6 Once the 1¾ hours have elapsed, stir the porcini and 300 ml (½ pint) of the reserved soaking liquid into the casserole, together with the artichokes. Cover, return the casserole to the oven and continue cooking for a further 30 minutes. Serve hot.

Individual Boeuf en Croûte

Serves 4

4 x 2.5-cm (1-in) thick fillet steaks

4 tablespoons olive oil

1 garlic clove, crushed

1 onion, chopped

175 g (6 oz) mushrooms, sliced

4 tablespoons medium-dry sherry

454-g (1-lb) packed frozen puff pastry, defrosted

1 tablespoon Moutarde de Meaux *or* Dijon mustard

salt and freshly ground black pepper

beaten egg, to seal and glaze

1 Pre-heat the oven to 220°C (425°F) Gas mark 7.

2 Trim the steaks, if necessary, into neat shapes. Heat the oil in a large frying pan, add the fillet steaks and cook for 1 minute on each side to seal. Transfer to kitchen paper and leave to cool.

3 Gently fry the garlic, onion and mushrooms in the oil in the same pan for 2 minutes. Add the sherry and cook for 3 minutes to reduce the liquid. Remove from the pan and leave to cool.

4 Roll out the pastry on a lightly floured surface and cut into 4 squares, each large enough to completely enclose a portion of steak.

5 Spread the cold steaks with the mustard and place in the centre of the pastry squares. Season with salt and pepper to taste and top each steak with the mushroom mixture.

6 Brush the pastry edges with beaten egg and draw up the corners to form neat parcels to completely enclose the meat (trimming the pastry if necessary) and pressing the edges together firmly to seal.

7 Place, join sides down, on a dampened baking sheet and brush with beaten egg to glaze. Using a sharp knife, lightly cut the top of each parcel in a lattice design, taking care not to cut right through the pastry. Decorate with pastry leaves made from the trimmings and brush with beaten egg to glaze.

8 Bake in the pre-heated oven for 20 minutes or until the pastry is golden brown. Serve hot.

Saltimbocca

Serves 4

4 veal escalopes, each no thicker than 5 mm (¼ in)

4 slices prosciutto, cut in half crossways

8 fresh sage leaves

freshly ground black pepper

3-4 tablespoons olive oil

15 g (½ oz) butter

5 tablespoons Marsala *or* medium sherry

300 ml (½ pint) beef stock

4 tablespoons double cream

1. Place the escalopes between two sheets of cling film and beat with a meat hammer until they are thin, then cut each one in half crossways to give 8 small escalopes.

2 Place a slice of prosciutto on each escalope. Top each one with a sage leaf and secure these in place with cocktail sticks. Season with pepper to taste.

3 Heat half the oil and butter in a large frying pan and fry 4 of the veal escalopes for 1–1½ minutes on each side. Remove from the pan and keep on one side while cooking the remainder in the same way, using the remaining oil and butter.

4 Return all the veal escalopes to the pan, pour the Marsala or sherry and the stock over the veal. Cover and cook gently for 3–4 minutes or until the veal is cooked through and tender.

5 Transfer the veal to a warm serving dish and keep warm. Add the cream to the mixture in the pan and boil to slightly reduce and thicken, then spoon the sauce over the veal and serve at once.

Roasted Mixed Peppers with Avocado and Olive Crème Fraîche

Steamed Mussels in Tomato Sauce

Fruited Goats' Cheese Salad

Provençal Chicken Pepper Tart

Veal Parmesan

Serves 4

4 veal escalopes, each weighing about 100 g (4 oz)

salt and freshly ground black pepper

50 g (2 oz) fine, fresh, white breadcrumbs

4 tablespoons freshly grated Parmesan cheese

1 egg, beaten

3–4 tablespoons extra-virgin olive oil

1 large beefsteak tomato, cut into 8 thin slices

175 g (6 oz) Mozzarella cheese, cut into 8 slices

1 Pre-heat the oven to 200°C (400°F) Gas mark 6.

2 Place each veal escalope between two sheets of cling film and beat with a meat hammer until they are thin. Season with salt and pepper to taste.

3 Mix the breadcrumbs with 2 tablespoons of Parmesan cheese and put on a plate.

4 Dip each escalope into the beaten egg to coat and then into the breadcrumb mixture, pressing the crumbs on firmly.

5 Heat the oil in a large frying pan and fry the escalopes for 3 minutes on each side, or until golden.

6 Place the escalopes in a single layer in a shallow, ovenproof dish. Top each with 2 slices of tomato and 2 slices of Mozzarella. Sprinkle with the remaining Parmesan and season once more with freshly ground pepper.

7 Bake in the pre-heated oven for 15 minutes, or until the topping has melted and is beginning to brown. Serve at once.

Herbed Rack of Lamb in a Pastry Case

Serves 4

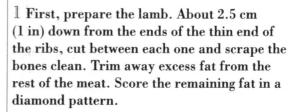

For the lamb

best end of lamb joint with 8 ribs, chined and backbone removed

salt and freshly ground black pepper

2 tablespoons olive oil

1 tablespoon chopped fresh parsley

1 tablespoon chopped fresh mint

1 garlic clove, crushed

½ x 454-g (1-lb) packet frozen puff pastry, defrosted

1 egg, beaten

For the red wine sauce

2 tablespoons olive oil

1 garlic clove, crushed

1 onion, finely chopped

175 ml (6 fl oz) red wine

150 ml (¼ pint) lamb *or* chicken stock

2 tablespoons crème fraîche

1 tablespoon redcurrant jelly

1 tablespoon chopped fresh mint

1 First, prepare the lamb. About 2.5 cm (1 in) down from the ends of the thin end of the ribs, cut between each one and scrape the bones clean. Trim away excess fat from the rest of the meat. Score the remaining fat in a diamond pattern.

2 Pre-heat the oven to 200°C (400°F) Gas mark 6.

3 Season the lamb joint with salt and pepper. Heat the oil in a frying pan and fry the lamb *well* on all sides (take about 15 minutes). Remove the lamb to kitchen paper to cool.

4 Mix 2 teaspoons juices from the pan with the parsley, mint and garlic and spread over the lamb. Reserve the remaining juices in the pan.

5 Roll out the pastry on a lightly floured surface and trim to a rectangle at least 13 cm (5 in) longer than the length of the joint and 5 cm (2 in) deeper than its height (excluding the bones); reserve the trimmings.

6 Brush the pastry with beaten egg. Place the cooled lamb joint in the centre and fold the pastry over to enclose it, leaving the ribs exposed. Press the pastry edges together firmly between each rib and seal neatly at each end.

7 Brush the pastry with beaten egg to glaze, then decorate with pastry leaves cut from the trimmings and brush these with beaten egg. Place the joint in a baking dish and bake in the pre-heated oven for 45–50 minutes, or until the pastry is golden brown and the lamb is cooked (cover the joint with foil during cooking once the pastry has browned to prevent it overbrowning).

8 Meanwhile, make the red wine sauce. Heat the oil in a saucepan with the reserved juices. Add the garlic and onion and fry gently for 10 minutes. Stir in the red wine, stock, crème fraîche, redcurrant jelly and mint. Bring to the boil and boil for 6–8 minutes to reduce slightly. Season to taste.

9 When ready, remove the joint from the oven and leave it to stand for 10 minutes. Slice in between the bones to the base of the joint and serve hot with the sauce, or cold on its own.

French Roast Lamb with Sorrel and Watercress Stuffing

Serves 6-8

5 tablespoons olive oil

1 onion, finely chopped

1 garlic clove, crushed

2 bunches watercress, stalks trimmed and leaves finely chopped

1 large handful of sorrel, stalks trimmed and leaves finely chopped

100 g (4 oz) fresh white breadcrumbs

1 egg, beaten

salt and freshly ground black pepper

1.4–1.6-kg (3–3½-lb) shoulder of lamb joint, boned

1 Pre-heat the oven to 190°C (375°F) Gas mark 5.

2 Heat 3 tablespoons oil in a saucepan, add the onion and garlic and cook gently for 3 minutes. Add the watercress and sorrel and cook for a further 3 minutes, stirring occasionally. Remove from the heat.

3 Add the breadcrumbs, egg and salt and pepper to taste, and mix well. Leave to cool.

4 Stuff the mixture into the cavity in the shoulder of lamb. Shape the lamb into a neat round and tie securely with string so it keeps a good shape during cooking.

5 Weigh the stuffed joint and calculate the cooking time, allowing 20 minutes per 450 g (1 lb), plus 30 minutes.

6 Heat the remaining oil in a roasting tin. Add the joint, brush with the oil and season with salt and pepper to taste. Roast for the calculated cooking time, basting occasionally.

7 Remove from the oven and leave to rest for 10 minutes before removing the string and carving (this dish is delicious served hot or cold).

Moroccan Lamb with Apricots

Serves 4

750 g (1½ lb) lean lamb, cubed

5 tablespoons olive oil

1 teaspoon ground cumin

pinch of freshly grated nutmeg

1 tablespoon chopped fresh mint

1 tablespoon chopped fresh coriander

2 garlic cloves, crushed

5 tablespoons orange juice

1 onion, halved and thinly sliced

2 tablespoons plain flour

100 g (4 oz) no-soak apricots

50 g (2 oz) muscatel raisins, stoned

150 ml (¼ pint) medium sherry

600 ml (1 pint) lamb *or* chicken stock

salt and freshly ground black pepper

natural yogurt and saffron rice, to serve

1 Place the lamb in a bowl with 2 tablespoons oil, cumin, nutmeg, mint, coriander, garlic and orange juice. Mix well, then cover and marinate in the fridge for several hours or overnight.

2 Pre-heat the oven to 180°C (350°F) Gas mark 4.

3 Heat the remaining oil in a large, flameproof casserole, add the onion and fry gently for 5 minutes, then remove from the pan.

4 Drain the lamb, reserving the marinade. Add the lamb to the hot oil in the casserole and brown over a high heat for a few minutes. Stir in the flour and cook for 1 minute. Add the reserved marinade, apricots, raisins, onion, sherry and stock. Season with salt and pepper to taste and bring to the boil.

5 Cover and cook in the pre-heated oven for 1¼ hours, or until the meat is tender. Drizzle with natural yogurt and serve hot with saffron rice.

Lamb Kibbeh with Two Dips
Serves 6

For the Lamb Kibbeh
225 g (8 oz) couscous

300 ml (½ pint) boiling water

4 tablespoons extra-virgin olive oil, plus extra for brushing

1 onion, finely chopped

1 garlic clove, crushed

½ teaspoon ground cinnamon

2 teaspoons ground cumin

450 g (1 lb) lean minced lamb

salt and freshly ground black pepper

sprigs of mint and lemon wedges, to garnish

For the garlic dip
100 g (4 oz) fresh, white breadcrumbs

1 tablespoon cold water

2 garlic cloves, crushed

salt and freshly ground black pepper

250 ml (8 fl oz) extra-virgin olive oil *or* olive oil

4 teaspoons lemon juice

1 tablespoon white wine vinegar

For the minted yogurt dip
150 ml (¼ pint) natural yogurt

3 tablespoons fresh soured cream

2 tablespoons chopped fresh mint

½ teaspoon caraway seeds

2 teaspoons lemon juice

freshly ground black pepper

1 Place the couscous in a bowl, add the boiling water and leave to soak for 15 minutes until all the liquid has been absorbed, stirring occasionally, and pre-heat the oven to 190°C (375°F) Gas mark 5.

2 Heat the oil in a frying pan, add the onion, garlic, cinnamon and cumin and cook gently for 2 minutes. Add the mixture to the soaked couscous and mix well. Add the lamb, season with salt and pepper to taste and mix well.

3 Divide the mixture evenly into 24 portions and form into balls or torpedo shapes. Place on a baking sheet and brush lightly with oil. Bake in the pre-heated oven for 35–40 minutes, or until golden and cooked through.

4 Meanwhile, make the garlic dip. Place the breadcrumbs, water and garlic in a blender or food processor and season well with salt and pepper to taste. Process until well mixed.

5 While the machine is running, add the oil, a little at a time and continue processing until all the oil has been added. Add the lemon juice and vinegar and process again to form a smooth, creamy sauce. Transfer the mixture to a serving dish.

6 To make the minted yogurt dip, place all the ingredients in a bowl and mix well. Season with pepper to taste and transfer to a serving bowl.

7 Arrange the Lamb Kibbeh on a serving platter with the two bowls of dip. Garnish with sprigs of mint and lemon wedges. Serve warm or cold.

Marinated Skewered Pork with Thyme and Bay

Serves 4

900 g (2 lb) pork tenderloin

5 tablespoons extra-virgin olive oil *or* olive oil

4 tablespoons dry white wine

2 tablespoons lemon juice

1 tablespoon chopped fresh thyme

1 garlic clove, crushed

salt and freshly ground black pepper

10 bay leaves, halved crossways

mixed pepper salad, to serve

1 Trim the pork, cut into 2-cm (¾-in) cubes and place in a shallow dish.

2 Mix the oil with the wine, lemon juice, thyme, garlic and salt and pepper to taste. Pour over the meat and stir well. Cover and marinate in the fridge for at least 3 hours, stirring occasionally.

3 Drain the cubes of meat (reserving the marinade) and thread on to 4 greased metal skewers with the halved bay leaves (allow 5 halved bay leaves per skewer). Do not pack the meat too tightly.

4 Cook under a hot grill for about 20 minutes, or until the pork is tender and cooked through, turning skewers frequently and brushing with the reserved marinade. Serve hot with a mixed pepper salad.

Fruited Pork Loin

Serves 4-6

1.5 kg (3 lb) loin of pork joint, chined and the skin finely scored

1 garlic clove, cut into thin strips

salt and freshly ground black pepper

3 tablespoons olive oil

100 g (4 oz) large, pitted prunes, soaked overnight in cold water

100 g (4 oz) no-soak apricots, soaked overnight with the prunes

2 onions, each cut into 6 wedges

8 sage leaves, shredded

2 sharp-flavoured eating apples, peeled, cored and each cut into 8 wedges

1 tablespoon lime *or* lemon juice

For the sauce

3 tablespoons plain flour

600 ml (1 pint) chicken stock

150 ml (¼ pint) reserved prune liquid

4 tablespoons Madeira

salt and freshly ground black pepper

1 Pre-heat the oven to 200°C (400°F) Gas mark 6.

2 Insert the strips of garlic under the skin and into the pork flesh. Season the joint with pepper and place in a roasting tin. Drizzle the skin with 2 tablespoons oil, then sprinkle the skin liberally with salt and rub in well. Roast the pork in the pre-heated oven for 1½ hours.

3 Meanwhile, drain the prunes and apricots, reserving the liquid. Mix the prunes and apricots with the onions, shredded sage leaves and apples and drizzle with the lime or lemon juice.

4 Add the fruit and onion mixture to the roasting tin once the 1½ hours have elapsed. Baste with the juices and the remaining oil, if necessary. Add 2 tablespoons stock and cook for a further 30–35 minutes, turning and basting the fruits and onions frequently with the juices until they are tender and the pork has cooked through.

5 Transfer the pork to a hot serving dish and surround with the fruit and onion mixture. Keep warm while making the sauce.

6 Strain off the juices from the roasting tin, retaining 2–3 tablespoons. Stir the flour into the tin and cook for 1 minute. Add the stock, 150 ml (¼ pint) reserved prune liquid and Madeira and bring to the boil, stirring. Simmer for 5 minutes, then season with salt and pepper to taste. Serve hot with the pork and basted fruits and onion.

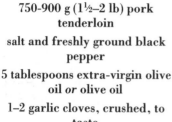

Peppered Pork Medallions with Mushroom Crème Fraîche

Serves 4-6

750-900 g (1½–2 lb) pork tenderloin

salt and freshly ground black pepper

5 tablespoons extra-virgin olive oil *or* olive oil

1–2 garlic cloves, crushed, to taste

2 onions, chopped

4 tablespoons brandy

350 g (12 oz) mushrooms, thinly sliced

1 tablespoon coarsely crushed green peppercorns

150 ml (¼ pint) crème fraîche

150 ml (¼ pint) double cream

300 ml (½ pint) chicken stock

chopped fresh parsley, to garnish

1 Trim the pork tenderloin, removing all sinews. Cut it, on the slant, into 2.5-cm (1-in) thick slices. Place the slices between two sheets of cling film and beat with a meat hammer until they are twice their original size. Season with salt and pepper to taste.

2 Heat the oil in a large frying pan and fry the pork medallions for 2–3 minutes on each side, or until cooked through. Transfer to a plate and keep warm.

3 Add the garlic, onions and brandy to the pan and cook for 2 minutes. Stir in the mushrooms, peppercorns, crème fraîche, cream and stock, and boil vigorously for 3–4 minutes, or until slightly reduced and thickened.

4 Add the pork medallions and heat through for 2 minutes. Serve hot, sprinkled with chopped parsley.

Grains, Beans and Pasta

Garlicky Bean and Potato Casserole

Serves 4

225 g (8 oz) dried haricot beans, soaked overnight in cold water

4 tablespoons extra-virgin olive oil *or* olive oil

100 g (4 oz) smoked streaky bacon, rinds removed and chopped (optional)

1 large onion, coarsely chopped

2 leeks, trimmed, halved and cut into 1-cm (½-in) thick slices

450 g (1 lb) new potatoes, scrubbed and quartered

2 garlic cloves, crushed

1 teaspoon cumin seeds

2 tablespoons tomato purée

1 tablespoon paprika

1 teaspoon sugar

1 litre (1¾ pints) chicken *or* vegetable stock

227-g (8-oz) tin chopped tomatoes

2 tablespoons chopped fresh coriander

salt and freshly ground black pepper

Greek yogurt, to serve

1 Drain the soaked beans and place in a saucepan. Add sufficient cold water to cover, then bring to the boil and boil rapidly for 10 minutes.

2 Meanwhile, heat the oil in a large flameproof casserole and fry the bacon, if using, onion, leeks and potatoes for about 10 minutes until potatoes are lightly golden.

3 Stir in the garlic, cumin seeds, tomato purée, paprika, sugar, stock and tomatoes. Bring to the boil, stirring.

4 Drain the beans and add to the casserole. Cover and simmer for 1½ hours, or until the beans are tender, stirring occasionally.

5 Stir in the coriander and season with salt and pepper to taste. Serve hot, topped with spoonfuls of Greek yogurt.

Smoked Sausage, Mixed Bean and Vegetable Casserole

Serves 6

4 tablespoons extra-virgin olive oil *or* olive oil

12 shallots

3 carrots, sliced

1 garlic clove, crushed

2 tablespoons plain flour

1.2 litres (2 pints) chicken stock

1 bay leaf

½ teaspoon dried oregano

450 g (1 lb) smoked pork sausage

3 courgettes, sliced

425-g (15-oz) tin cannellini beans, drained

225-g (8-oz) tin red kidney beans, drained

salt and freshly ground black pepper

flakes of fresh Parmesan cheese

warm, crusty bread, to serve

1 Heat the oil in a flameproof casserole, add the shallots and carrots and fry gently for 10 minutes.

2 Stir in the garlic and the flour and cook for 1 minute. Gradually add the stock and bring to the boil, stirring. Add the bay leaf and oregano, cover and simmer for 20 minutes.

3 Cut the sausage into chunky slices and add to the casserole. Stir in the courgettes and beans, then cover and continue cooking for a further 20 minutes.

4 Discard the bay leaf, add salt and pepper to taste and sprinkle liberally with flakes of Parmesan cheese. Serve with warm, crusty bread.

Spiced Chicken, Pepper and Lemon Couscous

Serves 4-6

225 g (8 oz) couscous

finely grated rind of 1 lemon

450 ml (¾ pint) cold water

6 tablespoons extra-virgin olive oil *or* olive oil

3 boneless chicken breasts, skinned, each one cut into 4 pieces

2 onions, chopped

2 leeks, sliced

2 garlic cloves, crushed

1½ teaspoons ground cumin

1½ teaspoons ground coriander

1.2 litres (2 pints) chicken stock

2 tablespoons tomato purée

2–3 teaspoons hot chilli sauce, to taste

440-g (15½-oz) tin chickpeas, drained

1 green pepper, de-seeded and cut into 1-cm (½-in) pieces

1 red pepper, de-seeded and cut into 1-cm (½-in) pieces

1 tablespoon lemon juice

1 tablespoon chopped fresh parsley

1 Put the couscous into a bowl, add the lemon rind and water and leave to soak for 15 minutes, or until the water has been absorbed.

2 Heat 4 tablespoons oil in a large saucepan, add the chicken and fry for 3-4 minutes until sealed all over. Remove from the pan and reserve.

3 Stir the onions and leeks into the pan and fry for 5 minutes, stirring frequently. Add the garlic and spices and cook for 1 minute, then stir in the stock, tomato purée and chilli sauce. Bring to the boil, stirring.

4 Line a metal steamer (it must fit the pan snugly) with muslin (or use a metal sieve or colander) and place over the pan. Put the couscous into the steamer (or sieve or colander), cover with a lid (if using a steamer, or cover the whole pan with foil to enclose the steam, if using a sieve or colander) and simmer for 20 minutes.

5 Stir the chickpeas, chicken, green and red pepper into the vegetable mixture in the saucepan. Re-cover with the couscous and cook for a further 20 minutes.

6 Spread the couscous on to a large serving dish, drizzle with the remaining oil and the lemon juice and fluff up with a fork.

7 Spoon the chicken and vegetable mixture over the couscous, sprinkle with the chopped parsley and serve hot.

Tabbouleh with Scallops in a Citrus-Sharp Dressing

Serves 6

For the Tabbouleh with Scallops

175 g (6 oz) bulgar wheat

warm water, to cover

3 tablespoons lemon juice

3 tablespoons extra-virgin olive oil

1 bunch spring onions, thinly sliced

2 tablespoons chopped fresh parsley

2 tablespoons chopped fresh mint

salt and freshly ground black pepper

450 g (1 lb) large scallops, cooked and shelled

For the dressing

juice of 1 lemon

juice of 1 lime

1 tablespoon chopped fresh dill

1 small garlic clove, crushed

2 shallots, finely chopped

150 ml (¼ pint) extra-virgin olive oil

salt and freshly ground black pepper

6 large, unshelled cooked prawns, sprigs of dill and slices of lemon and lime, to garnish

1 Put the bulgar wheat into a bowl, cover with the warm water and leave to soak for 30 minutes. Squeeze out any excess water and transfer the bulgar wheat to a bowl.

2 Add the lemon juice, olive oil, spring onions, parsley, mint and salt and pepper to taste. Mix well, cover and chill for at least 30 minutes, turning occasionally.

3 Meanwhile, slice the white parts of the scallops thinly, reserving the orange corals. Place the sliced scallops in a shallow dish.

4 Next, make the dressing. Whisk together the lemon and lime juices with the dill, garlic, shallots and 100 ml (4 fl oz) olive oil. Season liberally with salt and pepper. Pour the mixture over the scallop slices and leave to marinate for 15 minutes.

5 Heat the remaining oil in a saucepan, add the reserved corals and cook very briefly (for a few seconds only). Remove from the pan, slice in half and add to the dish with the scallops.

6 Place a portion of Tabbouleh on one side of 6 serving plates and arrange the scallop mixture on the other side. Garnish with prawns, sprigs of dill and slices of lemon and lime.

Roasted Sweet Peppers with Bulgar Wheat

Serves 6

For the pepper and bulgar

2 large yellow peppers

2 large orange peppers

2 large red peppers

175 g (6 oz) bulgar wheat

300 ml (½ pint) cold vegetable stock

150 ml (¼ pint) dry white wine

6 tablespoons extra-virgin olive oil, plus extra for greasing

1 large onion, chopped

2 garlic cloves, crushed

1–2 small, fresh, green chillies, de-seeded and chopped, to taste

finely grated rind and juice of 1 lemon

50 g (2 oz) sultanas *or* raisins *or* chopped no-soak apricots

50 g (2 oz) almonds, toasted and coarsely chopped

salt and freshly ground black pepper

For the marinade

150 ml (¼ pint) extra-virgin olive oil

juice of 3 limes

2 tablespoons cold cooking liquor (from the dish of cooked peppers)

1 tablespoon balsamic vinegar

1 tablespoon clear honey

salt and freshly ground black pepper

1 Slice the peppers in half lengthways, cutting through the stalks as well (they look attractive cut this way). Scoop out the seeds and membranes from each halved pepper, but leave the stalks on.

2 Place the peppers close together in a shallow, greased baking dish.

3 Put the bulgar wheat in a bowl and cover with the stock and wine. Leave to soak for 30 minutes. Drain the bulgar wheat in a sieve, pressing out the excess liquid and reserve it. Place the bulgar wheat in a bowl.

4 Heat 3 tablespoons oil in a saucepan, add the onion, garlic and chillies and fry gently for 15 minutes, stirring occasionally. Remove from the heat and pre-heat the oven to 180°C (350°F) Gas mark 4.

5 Add the onion mixture to the bulgar wheat, then stir in the remaining oil, lemon rind and juice, sultanas or raisins or apricots, almonds and salt and pepper to taste.

6 Spoon the mixture into the peppers and press lightly to firm to a neat shape. Add the reserved liquid (from soaking the bulgar wheat) to the dish. Cover the dish with greased foil then bake in the pre-heated oven for about 45 minutes, or until the peppers are tender.

7 Leave to cool, still covered with foil for several hours or overnight. Arrange the peppers on a serving dish.

8 To make the marinade, whisk the ingredients together and season with salt and pepper to taste. Spoon over the peppers and leave to marinate at room temperature for 1–2 hours before serving.

Asparagus, Wild Mushroom and Pine Nut Risotto

Serves 4

15-g (½-oz) packet dried ceps

300 ml (½ pint) warm water

225 g (8 oz) fresh asparagus spears

6 tablespoons olive oil

1 onion, chopped

1 garlic clove, crushed

225 g (8 oz) field mushrooms, sliced

350 g (12 oz) arborio (risotto) rice

150 ml (¼ pint) dry vermouth *or* white wine

900 ml (1½ pints) rich chicken *or* vegetable stock

salt and freshly ground black pepper

40 g (1½ oz) pine nuts, toasted

25–50 g (1–2 oz) Parmesan cheese, flaked

1 Rinse the dried mushrooms in a sieve under cold running water, then place in a bowl and cover with the warm water. Leave to soak for 20–30 minutes.

2 Cut off the woody part at the base of the asparagus stems, and, using a knife, scrape off the white part of the stems. Cut the asparagus spears diagonally into 3 or 4 pieces. Cook in a pan with enough boiling, salted water to cover for 8–10 minutes, or until just tender. Drain well.

3 Heat 4 tablespoons oil in a saucepan, add the onion, garlic and fresh mushrooms and fry gently for 5 minutes, or until soft.

4 Drain the soaked dried mushrooms in a muslin-lined sieve, reserving the liquid. Chop the mushrooms fairly finely. Add to the pan and cook for 3 minutes, stirring.

5 Add in the rice and cook for 2 minutes, stirring to coat all the grains in the oil.

6 Gradually add the reserved mushroom-soaking liquid and the vermouth or wine, then stir in a third of the stock and cook gently, stirring frequently until the stock is absorbed. Season with salt and pepper to taste.

7 When the rice becomes creamy, continue adding more stock, a ladleful at a time, as soon as each addition has been absorbed, stirring frequently. The mixture should cook for about 25–30 minutes, or until the rice is tender (you may not need to add all the stock).

8 Heat the remaining oil in a frying pan, add the asparagus and heat gently for 2–3 minutes.

9 Add the asparagus and pine nuts to the risotto and toss lightly. Sprinkle with the flaked Parmesan cheese and serve hot.

Paella Valenciana

Serves 4

4 boneless chicken breasts, with skin

5 tablespoons extra-virgin olive oil *or* olive oil

1 onion, chopped

1 green *or* red pepper, de-seeded and cut into strips

1 garlic clove, crushed

275 g (10 oz) arborio (risotto) rice

600 ml (1 pint) rich chicken stock

4 tomatoes, skinned, de-seeded and chopped

75 g (3 oz) frozen peas

2 pinches saffron strands, crushed

salt and freshly ground black pepper

150 ml (¼ pint) water

20 fresh mussels, cleaned (see page 35)

12 cooked, peeled tiger prawns

chopped fresh parsley, to garnish

1 Cut the chicken breasts in half crossways to give 8 neat pieces. Heat the oil in a large frying pan and fry the chicken pieces for 5 minutes until lightly golden all over. Remove from the pan and keep warm.

2 Add the onion, pepper and garlic to the pan and fry gently for 3 minutes. Stir in the rice, stirring until well coated with oil.

3 Stir in about a third of the stock, the tomatoes, peas and saffron and salt and pepper to taste. Mix well, then return the chicken to the pan and bring the mixture to the boil, stirring occasionally.

4 Cover and cook for 5 minutes or until the liquid has been absorbed. Add another third of the stock and cook for 5 more minutes. Once this liquid is absorbed, add the remaining stock and cook until the rice is tender and has absorbed all the liquid.

5 Meanwhile, put the water and mussels in a saucepan. Cover and bring to the boil and cook for 2–3 minutes, or until the mussels have opened and are cooked. Shake the pan occasionally during cooking. Strain and discard any mussels that remain closed.

6 Add the prawns and mussels to the rice mixture. Cover and heat through for 5 minutes. Serve hot, garnished with chopped parsley.

Aubergine and Tomato Lasagne
Serves 6

❧❦❧

2 large aubergines

salt

6 fresh (*or* dried) lasagne sheets

For the tomato sauce

150 ml (¼ pint) extra-virgin olive oil *or* olive oil

1 large Spanish onion, chopped

2 garlic cloves, crushed

2 celery sticks, thinly sliced

100 g (4 oz) mushrooms, sliced

400-g (14-oz) tin chopped tomatoes

4 tablespoons tomato purée

5 tablespoons red wine

1 teaspoon dried oregano

salt and freshly ground black pepper

For the cheese sauce

50 g (2 oz) butter

50 g (2 oz) plain flour

600 ml (1 pint) milk

100 g (4 oz) Mozzarella cheese, chopped

40 g (1½ oz) freshly grated Pecorino or Parmesan cheese

2 eggs, beaten

salt and freshly ground black pepper

❧❦❧

1 First, make the tomato sauce. Heat 4 tablespoons oil in a saucepan, add the onion, garlic and celery and fry gently for 5 minutes. Stir in the mushrooms, tomatoes, tomato purée, wine, oregano and salt and pepper to taste. Simmer, uncovered, for 15 minutes until thick, stirring frequently.

2 Meanwhile, cut the aubergines into 5-mm (¼-in) thick slices. Dissolve 1 tablespoon salt in a bowl containing 1.2 litres (2 pints) hot water. Add the aubergine slices and leave to soak for 15 minutes, weighed down with a plate to keep the slices submerged in the liquid.

3 Pre-heat the oven to 180°C (350°F) Gas mark 4.

4 Drain the aubergine and squeeze out excess moisture by pressing each slice between your hands and pat dry with kitchen paper. Brush the aubergine slices on both sides with oil and grill, turning frequently, until golden.

5 Meanwhile, if using dried lasagne that requires pre-cooking, cook it in a large pan of boiling, salted water according to the directions on the packet. Drain and leave to dry on a clean teatowel.

6 Make the cheese sauce. Melt the butter in a pan, add the flour and cook for 1 minute. Gradually stir in the milk and bring to the boil, stirring, then reduce the heat and simmer for 2 minutes, stirring all the time. Remove from the heat and stir in half the Mozzarella and Pecorino or Parmesan cheeses, then add the beaten eggs, season to taste and beat well together.

7 Place 2 of the lasagne sheets in a large,

greased, shallow, ovenproof dish and spread with half the tomato sauce. Cover with half the aubergine slices and top with half the cheese sauce.

8 Place another 2 lasagne sheets over the sauce and top with the remaining tomato mixture. Cover with the remaining aubergine slices and top with the remaining lasagne sheets.

9 Spread the remaining sauce on top and sprinkle with the remaining Mozzarella and Pecorino cheeses.

10 Bake in the pre-heated oven for 35–40 minutes until the topping has set and is golden. Leave to cool for 10 minutes, then cut into portions and serve hot.

Tagliatelle with a Fresh Herb and Parmesan Sauce

Serves 4

An extremely quick and delicious pasta dish.

275–350 g (10–12 oz) dried tagliatelle

4 egg yolks

8 tablespoons extra-virgin olive oil

2 garlic cloves, crushed

2 tablespoons chopped fresh basil

2 tablespoons chopped fresh oregano

2 tablespoons chopped fresh chives

75 g (3 oz) freshly grated Parmesan *or* Pecorino cheese

salt and freshly ground black pepper

1 Cook the pasta in a large pan of boiling, salted water for 8–10 minutes, or until *al dente* (tender but still a little firm to the bite).

2 Meanwhile, in a bowl mix together the egg yolks, oil, garlic, herbs, Parmesan or Pecorino cheese and salt and pepper to taste.

3 Drain the pasta, return to the pan and place over a very low heat. Add the herb and cheese mixture and mix with the pasta, lifting and stirring with 2 forks to mix the ingredients together (take care not to overheat the mixture – a few moments over heat should be sufficient to form a sauce for coating the pasta). Serve at once.

Capellini with Prawns, Broccoli and Red Pepper

Serves 4

1 red pepper

100 g (4 oz) broccoli

4 tablespoons extra-virgin olive oil *or* olive oil

1 onion, finely chopped

1 garlic clove, crushed

1 fresh chilli, de-seeded and chopped

275–350 g (10–12 oz) dried capellini or linguine or spaghetti

150 ml (¼ pint) single cream

2 tablespoons chopped fresh parsley

225 g (8 oz) cooked, peeled prawns

salt and freshly ground black pepper

1 Grill the pepper until the skin blisters and blackens. Place it in a sealed polythene bag and leave to cool slightly. Remove the skin and seeds and cut the pepper into thin slivers.

2 Cut the lower parts of the stems off the broccoli and divide into small, even-sized florets. Cut the stalks in half lengthways, then cut into slices. Cook the broccoli stalks in a little boiling salted water for 3 minutes. Add the florets and cook for a further 3 minutes. Drain.

3 Heat the oil in a saucepan, add the onion, garlic and chilli, and cook gently for 5 minutes, stirring occasionally.

4 Cook the pasta in a large pan of boiling, salted water for 8–10 minutes, or until *al dente* (tender but still a little firm to the bite).

5 Add the broccoli and pepper strips to the onion mixture and fry for 2 minutes, stirring. Add the cream, parsley, prawns and salt and pepper to taste, and mix well.

6 Drain the pasta and add to the pan. Stir and lift with 2 forks to mix the ingredients and heat through gently. Serve hot.

Vegetables

Sautéed Garlic Potatoes

Serves 4

900 g (2 lb) old (maincrop) potatoes, peeled and cut into 2.5-cm (1-in) pieces

5 tablespoons extra-virgin olive oil *or* olive oil

6 garlic cloves

salt and freshly ground black pepper

squeeze of lemon juice

2 tablespoons chopped mixed fresh chives and parsley

1 Rinse the potato pieces in a sieve under cold running water. Drain well and pat dry on kitchen paper.

2 Heat the oil in a large frying pan, add the potatoes, in a single layer if possible, and fry over a moderate heat for 5 minutes, stirring and turning constantly until lightly golden all over.

3 Add the garlic cloves and sprinkle with salt and pepper to taste. Cover the pan and cook very gently for about 15 minutes, shaking the pan and stirring the mixture occasionally.

4 Test the potatoes when crisp and golden (they should feel tender inside when pierced with a skewer).

5 Remove the garlic cloves and discard the skins. Crush the garlic, mix with the lemon juice, add to the potatoes and stir to mix. Heat through for 1–2 minutes, then transfer to a hot serving dish, sprinkle with the chives and parsley and serve at once.

Italian-Style Fennel with Spinach

Serves 4-6

6 tablespoons extra-virgin olive oil *or* olive oil, plus extra for greasing

1 large onion, chopped

2 garlic cloves, crushed

1 dried, red chilli, finely chopped

1 teaspoon dried oregano *or* dried mixed herbs

2 x 400-g (14-oz) tins chopped tomatoes

salt and freshly ground black pepper

450 g (1 lb) frozen leaf spinach, defrosted

2 large fennel bulbs

2 eggs, beaten

8 tablespoons fresh white *or* brown breadcrumbs

225 g (8 oz) Fontina cheese, sliced

25 g (1 oz) Pecorino cheese, grated

1 Pre-heat the oven to 180°C (350°F) Gas mark 4.

2 Heat 4 tablespoons oil in a saucepan, add the onion, garlic, chilli, oregano or mixed herbs and tomatoes. Simmer, uncovered, for 25–30 minutes, or until the sauce is really thick, stirring frequently. Season with salt and pepper to taste.

3 Meanwhile, cook the spinach, following the directions on the packet. Drain well in a sieve, pressing out as much moisture as possible. Coarsely chop the spinach and mix into the prepared sauce.

4 Trim the leaves off the fennel bulbs and reserve for garnishing. Cut the bases off the fennel bulbs and carefully separate the rest of the bulbs into layers. Blanch the layers in boiling, salted water for 10 minutes, or until just tender. Drain well and pat dry on kitchen paper.

5 Mix the beaten eggs and breadcrumbs into the spinach mixture and use to stuff the fennel layers firmly. Arrange the stuffed fennel in a shallow, greased ovenproof dish (using pieces of crumpled foil, if necessary, to keep the fennel upright during cooking).

6 Arrange the sliced Fontina cheese on top and sprinkle with the grated Pecorino. Drizzle with the remaining olive oil and sprinkle with pepper to taste.

7 Bake in the pre-heated oven for about 35–40 minutes, or until golden brown and tender. Garnish with the reserved fennel leaves and serve hot.

Sweet Onion and Gruyère Tart

Serves 6-8

For the pastry

225 g (8 oz) plain flour

pinch of salt

2 pinches of cayenne pepper

1 egg, beaten

4 tablespoons olive oil

3 tablespoons water

For the filling

2 tablespoons olive oil

2 large Spanish onions, halved and thinly sliced

3 eggs, beaten

150 ml (¼ pint) single cream

1 teaspoon wholegrain *or* Dijon mustard

salt and freshly ground black pepper

1 tablespoon chopped fresh chives

75 g (3 oz) Gruyère cheese, grated

1 First, make the pastry. Sift the flour, salt and cayenne into a bowl and make a well in the centre. Mix together the egg, oil and water, add to the well in the flour and mix vigorously with a fork to form a dough. Knead lightly and form into a ball. Cover with a damp cloth and leave to rest for 30 minutes.

2 Pre-heat the oven to 200°C (400°F) Gas mark 6.

3 Roll out the pastry on a lightly floured surface and use to line a 25-cm (10-in), loose-bottomed fluted flan tin set on a baking sheet. Trim the top edge and prick the base all over with a fork. Line with foil and fill with baking beans.

4 Bake in the pre-heated oven for 10 minutes. Remove the foil and beans and cook for a further 5 minutes. Remove from the oven.

5 Meanwhile, prepare the filling. Heat the oil in a frying pan, add the onions and fry gently for 10 minutes, stirring frequently. Remove from the heat and leave to cool slightly.

6 Beat the eggs with the cream and mustard and season with salt and pepper to taste.

7 Arrange the onions in the pastry case, pour the egg mixture on top and sprinkle with the chives and cheese.

8 Bake in the oven for 25–30 minutes, or until the filling is set and a rich golden brown. Serve warm or cold.

Chillied Mixed Mushrooms

Serves 4

750 g (1½ lb) mixed mushrooms (field, button, chestnut, oyster)

6 tablespoons olive oil

4 shallots, chopped

1–2 fresh, green chillies, to taste, de-seeded and chopped

1 teaspoon chopped fresh thyme

1 teaspoon chopped fresh marjoram

1 tablespoon chopped fresh parsley

finely grated rind of 1 lemon

2 teaspoons lemon juice

1 garlic clove, very finely chopped

salt and freshly ground black pepper

1 Trim the stalks of the mushrooms to neaten and cut the larger mushrooms in halves or quarters to make all the mushrooms roughly the same size.

2 Heat the oil in a large frying pan, add the mushrooms, shallots and chillies, shake the pan, cover tightly and cook gently for 8 minutes, shaking the pan frequently.

3 Uncover the pan and continue cooking over a high heat until all the liquid has evaporated and the mushrooms are sizzling.

4 Sprinkle with the herbs, lemon rind and juice, garlic and salt and pepper to taste. Heat through for 2 minutes. Serve hot.

Gratinéed New Potatoes with Tarragon Cream

Serves 4

900 g (2 lb) small new potatoes, scrubbed

300 ml (½ pint) double cream

2 sprigs of fresh tarragon

4 tablespoons olive oil

1 onion, chopped

1 garlic clove, crushed

salt and freshly ground black pepper

50–75 g (2–3 oz) Emmental cheese, grated

1 Pre-heat the oven to 200°C (400°F) Gas mark 6.

2 Cook the potatoes in lightly salted, boiling water for 10 minutes. Drain and cool slightly, then cut into chunky slices.

3 Place the cream and sprigs of tarragon in a saucepan, bring to the boil and boil for a few minutes to reduce the quantity by a third. Remove from the heat and discard the tarragon.

4 Heat the oil in a frying pan, add the onion and potato slices and fry for about 8 minutes or until lightly golden, turning frequently. Remove from the heat and stir in the garlic.

5 Transfer the mixture to a shallow, ovenproof dish and season liberally with salt and pepper to taste. Pour the cream over the potatoes and sprinkle with the cheese.

6 Bake in the pre-heated oven for about 15–20 minutes, or until golden and sizzling. Serve hot.

Ratatouille Gougère

Serves 6

For the Ratatouille

1 aubergine, quartered and sliced

2 courgettes, sliced

salt

6 tablespoons extra-virgin olive oil, plus extra for greasing

1 onion, halved and sliced

2 garlic cloves, crushed

1 green pepper, de-seeded and cut into strips

1 red pepper, de-seeded and cut into strips

225 g (8 oz) ripe tomatoes, skinned and chopped

1 tablespoon chopped fresh basil

1 tablespoon chopped fresh thyme

2 tablespoons tomato purée

freshly ground black pepper

50 g (2 oz) Gruyère *or* Cheddar cheese, grated

For the choux pastry

65 g (2½ oz) plain flour

pinch of salt

150 ml (¼ pint) cold water

45 g (1¾ oz) butter

2 eggs, beaten

50 g (2 oz) Gruyère *or* Cheddar cheese, finely diced

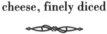

1 Place the aubergine and courgettes in layers in a colander or sieve (standing on a plate) and sprinkle each layer with salt, using about 2 teaspoons in total. Leave to stand for 30 minutes, then rinse under cold running water and pat dry with kitchen paper.

2 Heat the oil in a large saucepan, add the onion, garlic, peppers and tomatoes, and fry gently for 10 minutes.

3 Stir in the herbs and tomato purée and season with pepper to taste. Cover and cook gently for 30 minutes, stirring occasionally.

4 Meanwhile, pre-heat the oven to 200°C (400°F) Gas mark 6 and make the choux pastry. Sift the flour and salt on to a sheet of greaseproof paper. Put the water and butter in a saucepan and heat gently until the butter has melted (do not let the water boil before the butter has melted).

5 Bring to the boil, remove from the heat and immediately add the flour, all at once, and stir quickly with a wooden spoon until smooth. Return the saucepan to the heat for a few moments and beat well until the dough forms a ball and leaves the sides of the saucepan clean. Remove from the heat and cool slightly.

6 Gradually add the beaten eggs, beating well after each addition and until the mixture forms a shiny dough. Stir in the diced cheese, then spoon the mixture around the edges of a greased 23-cm (9-in) ovenproof flan dish.

7 Bake in the pre-heated oven for 30 minutes. Spoon the hot ratatouille mixture into the centre of the choux ring, sprinkle with the grated cheese and continue cooking for a further 15 minutes. Serve at once.

Braised French Beans and Tomatoes Provençal

Serves 4-6

350 g (12 oz) French beans, topped and tailed, if wished

4 tablespoons extra-virgin olive oil

2 garlic cloves, crushed

salt and freshly ground black pepper

3 shallots, sliced

6 tomatoes, halved

50 g (2 oz) fresh white breadcrumbs

2 tablespoons chopped fresh parsley

1 tablespoon chopped fresh thyme

1 Pre-heat the oven to 200°C (400°F) Gas mark 6.

2 Steam the French beans for 6 minutes and place in a shallow, ovenproof dish.

3 Mix the oil with the garlic and drizzle 1 tablespoon of it over the beans, then season with salt and pepper to taste.

4 Heat the remaining garlic oil in a frying pan and fry the shallots for 2 minutes, then add the tomatoes and fry briefly on both sides.

5 Arrange the shallots and the tomatoes, cut sides up, on top of the beans and season with salt and pepper to taste. Mix the breadcrumbs with the herbs and sprinkle on top. Drizzle with the garlic oil remaining in the pan.

6 Bake in the pre-heated oven for 15–20 minutes until golden brown. Serve hot.

Aubergine and Tomato Parmigiana
Serves 4

2 aubergines, cut into 1-cm
(½-in) thick slices

salt

150 ml (¼ pint), plus
1 tablespoon extra-virgin olive
oil

2 onions, chopped

2 garlic cloves, crushed

400-g (14-oz) tin chopped
tomatoes

1 tablespoon chopped fresh
oregano *or* marjoram

2 tablespoons tomato purée

freshly ground black pepper

175 g (6 oz) Mozzarella cheese,
chopped

3 tablespoons freshly grated
Parmesan cheese

1 Pre-heat the oven to 190°C (375°F) Gas mark 5.

2 Place the aubergine slices in a colander or sieve (standing on a plate) and sprinkle with 2 teaspoons salt. Leave for 30 minutes.

3 Rinse the aubergines under cold running water and pat dry on kitchen paper.

4 Heat 3 tablespoons oil in a large saucepan and fry the onions and garlic for 2 minutes. Stir in the tomatoes, oregano or marjoram, tomato purée and salt and pepper to taste. Bring to the boil, then reduce the heat and cook for 10 minutes, stirring occasionally.

5 Meanwhile, heat 3 tablespoons oil in a large frying pan, add about half the aubergine slices and fry for 3 minutes on each side until golden. Remove from the pan and reserve. Repeat this process using the remaining oil and aubergine slices.

6 Layer the aubergines and the tomato mixture in an ovenproof dish. Cover with Mozzarella cheese and sprinkle with the Parmesan and pepper to taste. Drizzle with the remaining 1 tablespoon oil.

7 Bake in the pre-heated oven for 35–40 minutes or until the topping is golden brown. Serve hot.

Marinated Artichokes with Peppers and Olives

Serves 4-6

2 large red peppers

397-g (14-oz) tin artichoke hearts, drained and quartered

2 red onions, quartered and thinly sliced

175 g (6 oz) pitted black olives *or* a mixture of black and green olives

150 ml (¼ pint) extra-virgin olive oil

2 tablespoons sherry *or* white wine vinegar

1 garlic clove, crushed

finely grated rind and juice of 1 lemon

2 teaspoons caster sugar

2 tablespoons chopped fresh chives

salt and freshly ground black pepper

warm, crusty bread, to serve

1 Place the peppers under a hot grill until the skins blister and blacken. Place them in a polythene bag, seal and leave until cool enough to handle.

2 Carefully peel off the skins, discarding the stalks and seeds. Cut the peppers into 1-cm (½-in) pieces and place in a bowl with the artichokes, onions and olives.

3 In another bowl, whisk together the oil, sherry or vinegar, garlic, lemon rind and juice, sugar and chives. Pour the mixture over the prepared vegetables and olives, add salt and pepper to taste and mix together lightly.

4 Cover and marinate in the fridge for at least 4 hours, stirring occasionally.

5 Allow to come to room temperature before serving with warm crusty bread to mop up all the delicious juices.

Pancetta-Stuffed Mushrooms

Serves 8

For the mushrooms

8 large field mushrooms

6 tablespoons olive oil, plus extra for greasing

1 large onion, finely chopped

2 garlic cloves, crushed

175 g (6 oz) pancetta *or* smoked streaky bacon, rinds removed and chopped

150 g (5 oz) fresh brown *or* white breadcrumbs

6 sage leaves, finely shredded

1 egg, beaten

salt and freshly ground black pepper

75 g (3 oz) Fontina *or* Gruyère cheese, finely grated

1 tablespoon grated Pecorino *or* Parmesan cheese

3 tablespoons dry white wine

3 tablespoons water

For the fried bread

olive oil, for frying

8 x 7.5-cm (3-in) rounds of white bread

1 garlic clove, halved

1 Pre-heat the oven to 190°C (375°F) Gas mark 5.

2 Peel the mushrooms. Remove the stalks and coarsely chop them. Brush the mushrooms all over with some oil and arrange, open sides up, in a shallow, greased, ovenproof dish.

3 Heat 4 tablespoons oil in a frying pan, add the onion, garlic, chopped mushroom stalks and pancetta or bacon and fry gently for 6 minutes, stirring frequently.

4 Remove from the heat and stir in 100 g (4 oz) breadcrumbs, sage, beaten egg and salt and pepper to taste and mix well. Divide the mixture into eight portions and spoon on to the open sides of the mushrooms, pressing the stuffing firmly to give a neat shape.

5 Mix the cheeses with the remaining breadcrumbs and sprinkle over the mushrooms. Drizzle with the remaining oil and add the wine and water to the dish.

6 Cover with greased foil and bake in the pre-heated oven for 15 minutes, then uncover and continue cooking for a further 10–15 minutes, or until the mushrooms are tender and the topping is crisp and golden, occasionally basting the mushrooms (but not the stuffing) with the juices in the dish.

7 Just before serving, prepare the bread. Heat some oil in a frying pan, add the garlic and fry gently for 30 seconds, then remove from the pan. Add the bread and fry until golden brown on each side. Drain on kitchen paper.

8 To serve, set a mushroom on each piece of fried bread and serve at once.

Barbecues

Marinated Swordfish Cooked in Vine Leaves

Serves 4

For the swordfish

4 x 150–175-g (5–6-oz) swordfish steaks

6 tablespoons extra-virgin olive oil *or* olive oil

2 tablespoons lemon *or* lime juice

1 teaspoon crushed black peppercorns

salt

4 large *or* 8 small vine leaves

lemon and lime wedges, to garnish

For the relish

6 spring onions, finely chopped

½ x 285-g (10½-oz) jar pepperoni (sliced yellow and red peppers in oil), drained and chopped

150 ml (¼ pint) fromage frais

1 tablespoon lemon *or* lime juice

freshly ground black pepper

1 Place the swordfish steaks in a large, shallow dish. Whisk the oil with the lemon or lime juice, crushed peppercorns and salt to taste. Pour over the fish, cover and leave to marinate in the fridge for at least 30 minutes.

2 Remove the fish from the marinade (reserving the marinade) and place each steak in the centre of a vine leaf. Wrap to enclose the fish and secure in place with fine string.

3 Place the fish on a greased barbecue rack and cook over a barbecue for about 15 minutes, or until the fish is cooked and flakes easily, turning and basting frequently with the reserved marinade.

4 Meanwhile, prepare the relish. Mix the ingredients together in a bowl and season with pepper to taste.

5 Garnish the fish with lemon and lime wedges and serve hot with spoonfuls of the pepperoni relish.

Red Mullet with Dill and Pink Grapefruit

Serves 4

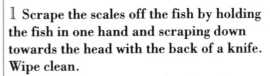

4 x 350–400-g (12–14-oz) red mullet, cleaned

4 tablespoons olive oil

8 sprigs of dill *or* parsley

salt and freshly ground black pepper

1 pink grapefruit

1 tablespoon chopped fresh dill *or* parsley

1 Scrape the scales off the fish by holding the fish in one hand and scraping down towards the head with the back of a knife. Wipe clean.

2 Brush each fish inside and out with oil. Place 2 sprigs of dill or parsley inside each one and season with salt and pepper.

3 Lay each fish on a piece of greased greaseproof paper placed over a piece of foil (all need to be large enough to wrap each fish loosely).

4 Pare the peel from the grapefruit thinly (taking care not to include the bitter white pith) and shred it very finely. Place in a pan, cover with water and boil for 3–4 minutes. Drain and reserve.

5 Squeeze the juice from the grapefruit and drizzle over the fish. Sprinkle with the grapefruit shreds and chopped dill or parsley. Fold up the greaseproof and foil to form neat parcels that completely enclose the fish, leaving a 2.5-cm (1-in) space over the fish to allow steam to circulate during cooking.

6 Arrange the parcels on a barbecue rack and barbecue for about 15 minutes, or until the fish is cooked and flakes easily (do not turn the parcels over during cooking). Serve hot.

Chargrilled Tiger Prawns
Serves 4-6

30 large, raw, fresh or frozen tiger prawns, unshelled but with heads removed, and defrosted if frozen

juice of 2 lemons

3 tablespoons medium dry sherry

2 teaspoons clear honey

2 small, dried chillies, finely chopped

salt

½ garlic clove

150 ml (¼ pint) extra-virgin olive oil *or* olive oil

wedges of lemon, to garnish

Aïoli (see page 114), to serve

1 Shell the prawns, leaving the tail shells intact (these look pretty for serving) and devein them. Place the prawns in a shallow dish.

2 In a bowl, mix together the lemon juice, sherry, honey and chillies and drizzle over the prawns. Season with salt to taste. Cover and leave to marinate in the fridge for at least 1 hour.

3 Meanwhile, place the garlic in the oil and leave for at least 1 hour to flavour the oil.

4 Dip the prawns in the oil, arrange on a barbecue rack and barbecue for 3–5 minutes, turning and brushing frequently with the remaining oil until the prawns turn pink and are tender and cooked.

5 Garnish with wedges of lemon and serve hot with Aïoli for dipping.

Peppered Tomato Steak en Brochette

Serves 4

For the steak

450 g (1 lb) rump steak,
trimmed and cut into 2.5-cm
(1-in) pieces

1 large red pepper, de-seeded
and cut into 2.5-cm (1-in)
pieces

1 large onion, quartered

For the marinade

1 fresh, green chilli, de-seeded

227-g (8-oz) tin tomatoes

2 tablespoons tomato purée

1 tablespoon vinegar

3 tablespoons olive oil

1 garlic clove

salt

1 teaspoon black peppercorns,
coarsely crushed

1 First prepare the marinade. Place the chilli, tomatoes, tomato purée, vinegar, oil and garlic in a blender or food processor and process to a smooth purée. Transfer the mixture to a saucepan, bring to the boil and simmer for 2 minutes.

2 Pour the marinade into a shallow dish, season with salt and add the crushed peppercorns. Leave to cool.

3 Add the steak, red pepper and onion quarters to the marinade. Cover and leave to marinate in the fridge for at least 4 hours.

4 Remove the steak, pepper and onions from the marinade, reserving the marinade. Separate the onion quarters into layers.

5 Thread the meat on to 4 oiled metal skewers, alternating with the pieces of red pepper and onion layers.

6 Arrange on a barbecue rack and barbecue for about 15 minutes, turning and basting frequently with the marinade. Serve hot.

Spiced Pork Skewers
Serves 4

450 g (1 lb) pork tenderloin
2 garlic cloves, crushed
½ teaspoon ground coriander
½ teaspoon ground cumin
½ teaspoon chilli powder
3 tablespoons olive oil
100 ml (3½ fl oz) orange juice
1 tablespoon soft brown sugar
salt

1 Cut the tenderloin lengthways into 4 slices. Mix the garlic with the coriander, cumin, chilli powder and 2 tablespoons oil and spread the mixture over the slices of pork.

2 Cut each pork slice into 4 long strips and thread on to 4 oiled bamboo skewers. Cover and leave to marinate in the fridge for at least 2 hours.

3 Arrange the skewers in a roasting tin (or similar tin for placing over a barbecue) and drizzle with the remaining oil.

4 Cook over the barbecue for 5 minutes, turning frequently until beginning to brown. Add the orange juice and sugar and season with salt to taste. Cover the tin with foil and simmer for 10 minutes.

5 Transfer the skewers to a hot serving plate and keep warm. Cook the orange juice mixture until syrupy, then drizzle over the skewers and serve hot.

Barbecued Chicken with Hot Red Sauce

Serves 4

4 chicken quarters

For the marinade

finely grated rind and juice of
1 lemon

finely grated rind and juice of
1 lime

2 tablespoons clear honey

4 tablespoons extra-virgin
olive oil *or* olive oil

salt and freshly ground black
pepper

1 teaspoon dried mixed herbs

For the sauce

3 tablespoons olive oil

1 garlic clove, crushed

450 g (1 lb) ripe tomatoes

1 tinned pimento, chopped

2 teaspoons paprika

½ teaspoon Tabasco sauce

1 Place the chicken quarters in a shallow dish.

2 Mix the marinade ingredients together and pour over the chicken. Cover and leave to marinate in the fridge for 2 hours.

3 Remove the chicken portions from the marinade (reserve the marinade) and arrange on a barbecue rack. Barbecue for about 15–20 minutes on each side, basting frequently with the marinade. Pierce through to the bone with a sharp, pointed knife to make sure that the chicken is cooked (if the juices run clear, it is ready, but, if the juices are pink, continue cooking for a further few minutes, then test again).

4 Meanwhile, make the sauce. Heat the oil in a frying pan, add the garlic, tomatoes, pimento, paprika and Tabasco, and cook gently for 10 minutes, stirring frequently. Purée the mixture in a blender or food processor and place in a flameproof serving dish. Keep warm on the side of the barbecue and serve hot with the chicken.

Pancetta-Wrapped Corn Cobs
Serves 4-6

4 fresh corn cobs, trimmed and husks removed, *or* frozen

24 slices pancetta *or* 12 streaky bacon rashers, rinds removed

4 tablespoons olive oil

1 garlic clove, crushed

½ teaspoon paprika

2 teaspoons balsamic vinegar

1 tablespoon chopped fresh parsley

1 tablespoon clear honey

salt

1 Cook the corn cobs in a saucepan of boiling water for 10 minutes (or follow the instructions on the packet if using frozen corn cobs). Drain and place on kitchen paper. Leave to cool slightly, then cut into 3 smaller pieces.

2 Wrap 2 slices of pancetta or bacon around each little corn cob and secure with small pieces of wooden cocktail stick (if using bacon, place on a board and use a knife to stretch each rasher to double its length; cut each one in half crossways to give 24 rashers and use in the same way as pancetta).

3 Whisk the oil with the garlic, paprika, vinegar, parsley and honey.

4 Arrange the wrapped corn cobs on a barbecue rack. Generously brush with the oil mixture and cook for 5–8 minutes, or until heated through and the pancetta or bacon is beginning to char, turning and brushing frequently with the oil mixture. Move corn to the side of the barbecue if it begins to brown too quickly.

5 Remove the cocktail sticks and arrange the corn cobs on a hot serving dish. Sprinkle with salt and serve at once with corn cob holders.

Crisp Potato Skins with Soured Cream Dip

Serves 6-8

For the potatoes

8 potatoes, each weighing about 100 g (4 oz), scrubbed

150 ml (¼ pint) olive oil, for frying

coarse salt, for serving

For the dip

150 ml (¼ pint) fresh soured cream *or* fromage frais

4 spring onions, finely chopped

1 garlic clove, crushed

2 tablespoons barbecue relish

salt and freshly ground black pepper

---

1 Pre-heat the oven to 200°C (400°F) Gas mark 6. Bake the potatoes in the oven for 45 minutes to 1 hour or until soft.

2. Meanwhile, make the dip. Mix the soured cream or fromage frais with the spring onions, garlic, barbecue relish and salt and pepper to taste. Transfer to a serving bowl, cover and chill until required.

3 Remove the potatoes from the oven and cut in half lengthways. Scoop out the flesh, leaving 1-cm (½-in) layer of potato on the skins. Cut each one in half lengthways.

4 Heat the oil in a deep frying pan (suitable for cooking on the barbecue) and fry the potato skins for 2–3 minutes, or until crisp and golden, turning frequently.

5 Drain on kitchen paper, sprinkle with salt and serve hot with the chilled dip.

Barbecued Vegetables

Serves 6-8

3 fennel bulbs, trimmed and halved lengthways

3 red onions, halved (through the root to keep the layers together)

12 cherry tomatoes, left whole

3 yellow peppers, halved lengthways through the stalks and de-seeded

6 courgettes, trimmed and cut diagonally in half

12 okra

150 ml (¼ pint) extra-virgin olive oil

2 garlic cloves, crushed

2 tablespoons chopped fresh marjoram

1 tablespoon soft brown sugar

salt and freshly ground black pepper

1 Cook the halved fennel bulbs and red onions in separate pans of lightly salted boiling water for 10 minutes. Drain well and pat dry with kitchen paper.

2 Thread the tomatoes on to an oiled skewer. Arrange all the vegetables in a large dish.

3 Mix the oil with the garlic, marjoram, sugar and salt and pepper to taste, and brush all over the vegetables.

4 Place the pepper halves, cut sides up, on a barbecue rack with the fennel, onions, courgettes and okra and cook for about 10–15 minutes, or until lightly charred and tender, turning and brushing frequently with the remaining oil mixture.

5 Add the skewered tomatoes to the barbecue rack about 5 minutes before the end of cooking, turning until the skins are beginning to blister and the tomatoes are only just cooked through.

6 Serve the vegetables hot, or keep them warm on the side of the barbecue, if necessary.

Greek-Style Cheese Kebabs

Serves 4

1 aubergine, cut into 2.5-cm
(1-in) thick slices, then each
quartered

2 green peppers, de-seeded
and cut into 2.5-cm (1-in)
squares

8 spring onion bulbs

3 nectarines, quartered and
stoned

450 g (1 lb) feta *or* halloumi
cheese, cut into 16 cubes

150 ml (¼ pint) extra-virgin
olive oil

1½ tablespoons chopped fresh
oregano

1½ tablespoons lemon juice

salt and freshly ground black
pepper

1 Put the aubergine, peppers, spring onion
bulbs, nectarine quarters and the cheese into
a dish.

2 In a bowl, mix together the oil, oregano,
lemon juice and salt and pepper to taste, and
pour over the ingredients in the dish. Toss
lightly to ensure everything is coated in the
mixture.

3 Thread the ingredients alternately on to
4 long, or 8 short, oiled metal skewers.

4 Arrange on a barbecue rack and barbecue
for about 10 minutes until the ingredients are
tender and lightly charred, turning and
brushing frequently with the oil mixture
remaining in the dish. Serve hot.

Microwave Recipes

All the recipes in this chapter have been tested using a 650–700-watt microwave, but can also be cooked using 500–600-watt microwaves by making adjustments to the cooking times (see the manufacturer's instructions).

Peperonata

Serves 4-6

5 tablespoons extra-virgin olive oil

1 garlic clove, crushed

1 onion, halved and very finely sliced

1 red pepper, de-seeded and cut into thin strips

1 green pepper, de-seeded and cut into thin strips

1 yellow pepper, de-seeded and cut into thin strips

6 tomatoes, skinned and chopped

salt and freshly ground black pepper

2 teaspoons sugar

1 Place the oil, garlic, onion and peppers in a large ovenproof casserole or bowl and mix well. Cover and microwave on High for 8–10 minutes or until softened, stirring frequently.

2. Add the tomatoes, salt and pepper to taste and the sugar. Mix well, cover and microwave on High for about 10 minutes or until the mixture is cooked through, stirring frequently. Serve warm or cold, but not chilled.

Creamy Aubergine Dip

Serves 6

900 g (2 lb) aubergines

salt

4 tablespoons water

2 garlic cloves, crushed

3 shallots

6 tablespoons extra-virgin olive oil

juice of ½ a lemon

1–2 tablespoons tahini (sesame cream), to taste

freshly ground black pepper

chopped fresh parsley, to garnish

warm fingers of pitta bread, to serve

1 Trim and peel the aubergines, then dice the flesh and place in a colander or sieve (standing on a plate). Sprinkle with 2 teaspoons salt and leave to stand for 30 minutes.

2 Rinse the aubergine under cold running water and pat dry with kitchen paper.

3 Put the aubergine into a large, ovenproof bowl and add the water. Partially cover and microwave on High for about 15 minutes, or until the aubergine is soft, stirring three times during cooking. Drain the aubergine in a sieve and leave to cool slightly.

4 Transfer the aubergine to a blender or food processor, add the garlic and shallots and blend to a smooth purée. Gradually add 5 tablespoons of the oil, drop by drop, then stir in the lemon juice and tahini and season with salt and pepper to taste.

5 Turn the mixture into a serving bowl and drizzle with the remaining oil. Sprinkle with parsley and serve with warm fingers of pitta bread.

Fennel and Courgettes à la Grecque

Serves 4

2 fennel bulbs

4 tablespoons extra-virgin olive oil *or* olive oil

1 leek, halved and shredded

2 garlic cloves, crushed

150 ml (¼ pint) dry white wine

2 tablespoons tomato purée

finely grated rind and juice of 1 lemon

2 courgettes, sliced

1 tablespoon shredded basil leaves

2 teaspoons caster sugar

salt and freshly ground black pepper

crusty bread, to serve

1 Trim the roots and stalk ends off the fennel bulbs and reserve the feathery fronds for garnishing. Quarter the bulbs and slice them thinly.

2 Put the oil, leek and garlic into a large, ovenproof casserole, cover and microwave on High for 7 minutes.

3 Add the sliced fennel, wine, tomato purée and lemon rind and juice. Partially cover and microwave on High for 8 minutes until boiling.

4 Stir well, add the sliced courgettes, basil, sugar and salt and pepper to taste. Cover and microwave on High for 2 minutes.

5 Reduce the setting to Low and microwave for about 15 minutes, stirring occasionally until all the vegetables are just tender.

6 Garnish with the reserved fennel fronds and serve warm with crusty bread.

Creamed Celery Soup with Brie

Serves 4

3 tablespoons olive oil

1 head of celery, trimmed and thinly sliced

1 onion, finely chopped

1 potato, thinly sliced

900 ml (1½ pints) chicken stock, hot

300 ml (½ pint) creamy milk

salt and freshly ground black pepper

150 ml (¼ pint) double cream

chopped fresh chives, to garnish

75 g (3 oz) firm Brie, cut into thin slivers

1 Put the oil into a large, ovenproof bowl and add the celery, onion and potato. Mix well, then cover and microwave on High for about 8 minutes or until the vegetables soften, stirring frequently.

2 Add the hot stock, milk and salt and pepper to taste. Partially cover the bowl and microwave on High for about 20 minutes or until the celery is very tender.

3 Leave the soup to cool slightly, then purée until smooth in a blender or food processor. Return the soup to the bowl, stir in the cream and reheat on High for 3-4 minutes.

4 Ladle the hot soup into warmed soup bowls, sprinkle with the chives and float the slivers of cheese on top.

Italian Prawns with Pasta

Serves 4

350 g (12 oz) dried tagliatelle

1.75 litres (3 pints) boiling water

salt

3 tablespoons extra-virgin olive oil *or* olive oil

1 garlic clove, crushed

1 fresh, green chilli, de-seeded and finely chopped

1 onion, finely chopped

227-g (8-oz) tin chopped tomatoes

3 tablespoons red wine

½ teaspoon dried oregano *or* marjoram

freshly ground black pepper

350 g (12 oz) cooked, peeled prawns

1 tablespoon chopped fresh parsley

2 tablespoons freshly grated *or* flaked Parmesan

1 Place the pasta in a 2.5-litre (4½-pint) ovenproof bowl. Pour the boiling water over the pasta and add a little salt to taste and 1 teaspoon of the oil. Cover and microwave on High for 7 minutes. Leave to stand, covered, for 5 minutes until it has cooked but is *al dente* (tender but still a little firm to the bite). Drain well and turn into a serving dish.

2 Place 2 tablespoons of the oil in a medium, ovenproof casserole or bowl, add the garlic, chilli and onion and microwave on High for 3 minutes.

3 Stir in the tomatoes, wine, herbs and salt and pepper to taste. Cover and microwave on High for 8 minutes, stirring halfway through cooking.

4 Add the prawns, mix well, three-quarters cover and microwave on High for a further 3 minutes or until heated through.

5 Toss the pasta with the remaining oil and the parsley. Microwave on High for 1 minute. Pour the sauce over the pasta and sprinkle with the grated or flaked Parmesan cheese.

Pasta and Steak in Cream Sauce
Serves 4-6

350 g (12 oz) dried pasta shapes

1.75 litres (3 pints) boiling water

salt

4 tablespoons, plus 1 teaspoon, olive oil

450 g (1 lb) rump *or* sirloin steak, cut into thin strips about 2.5-cm (1-in) long

1 large onion, finely chopped

175 g (6 oz) mushrooms, thinly sliced

2 tablespoons plain flour

150 ml (¼ pint) hot beef stock

1 tablespoon tomato purée

150 ml (¼ pint) crème fraîche

freshly ground black pepper

1 Place the pasta shapes in a 2.5-litre (4½-pint) ovenproof bowl. Pour the boiling water over the pasta and add a little salt and 1 teaspoon oil. Mix well, cover and microwave on High for 7 minutes. Leave to stand, covered, for 5 minutes, or until it has cooked, but is still *al dente* (tender but a little firm to the bite). Drain well.

2 Pre-heat a browning dish, following the manufacturer's instructions, adding 2 tablespoons oil for the last 20 seconds.

3 Without removing the dish from the oven, add half the steak strips, turning and pressing them flat against the surface, using a fish slice. Microwave on High for 30 seconds, or until sealed all over.

4 Using a draining spoon, remove the meat and set aside. Pour off the juices and reserve. Wipe out the hot browning dish with several sheets of kitchen paper, then heat it again as before, adding 2 tablespoons oil for the last 20 seconds.

5 Add remaining steak strips and cook as before. Using a draining spoon, remove the steak from the dish and reserve with the first batch.

6 Add the reserved juices to the dish and stir in the onion. Cover and microwave on High for 3 minutes. Add the mushrooms and microwave on High for 1–2 minutes, or until the vegetables are soft.

7 Stir in the flour and microwave on High for 1 minute, stirring twice. Stir in the hot stock, tomato purée and crème fraîche. Cover and microwave on High for 2–3 minutes, or until hot, stirring twice.

8 Add the steak strips and any juices that have drained from them to the dish, then cover and microwave on High for 2 minutes, or until piping hot, stirring once or twice. Thin the consistency of the sauce with extra hot stock, if necessary. Season with salt and pepper to taste.

9 Pour the sauce over the pasta and mix gently. Cover and microwave on High for a further 2 minutes, or until the pasta is heated through.

Lemony Trout with Almonds

Serves 4

3 tablespoons olive oil, plus extra for greasing

15 g (½ oz) butter

50 g (2 oz) flaked almonds

1 onion, finely chopped

1 garlic clove, crushed

65 g (2½ oz) fresh white breadcrumbs

15 g (½ oz) ground almonds

1 tablespoon chopped fresh parsley

1 tablespoon chopped fresh chives

finely grated rind and juice of 1½ lemons

salt and freshly ground black pepper

4 trout, each weighing about 225 g (8 oz), cleaned

1 Place 2 tablespoons of the oil and the butter in a medium ovenproof bowl with the flaked almonds and microwave on High for 1½ minutes, stirring twice. Using a draining spoon, remove the almonds from the bowl and reserve.

2 Add the remaining oil, onion and garlic to the bowl, cover and microwave on High for 8 minutes.

3 Stir in the breadcrumbs, ground almonds, parsley, chives, rind and juice of 1 lemon and salt and pepper to taste; mix well.

4 Fill each trout with the stuffing. Carefully slash the skin of each trout 2 or 3 times on each side and arrange in a large, greased, ovenproof dish. Brush fish with the remaining lemon rind and juice.

5 Cover and microwave on High for 8–10 minutes, turning the trout over and repositioning them halfway through cooking.

6 Leave to stand, covered, for 5 minutes before serving, sprinkled with the flaked almonds.

Mediterranean Chicken

Serves 4

3 tablespoons olive oil

4 chicken joints

1 green pepper, de-seeded and diced

1 Spanish onion, halved and finely sliced

2 garlic cloves, crushed

400-g (14-oz) tin chopped tomatoes

2 tablespoons tomato purée

½ teaspoon dried oregano

salt and freshly ground black pepper

1 tablespoon cornflour

2 tablespoons medium-dry sherry *or* wine *or* water

25–50 g (1–2 oz) stuffed olives, sliced

1 Pre-heat a browning dish to maximum, following the manufacturer's instructions, adding the oil for the last 20 seconds.

2 Without removing the dish from the oven, quickly place the chicken joints, skin sides down, in the hot oil. Microwave on High for 3 minutes, then turn the chicken over.

3 Add the pepper, onion, garlic, tomatoes, tomato purée, oregano and salt and pepper to taste; mix well. Cover and microwave on High for 12 minutes, repositioning the chicken twice during cooking.

4 Reduce the setting to Low and microwave for a further 10 minutes, or until the chicken is tender.

5 Remove the chicken to a hot serving dish and keep warm. Blend the cornflour to a smooth paste with the sherry, wine or water and stir into the tomato mixture. Microwave on High for 5 minutes, stirring twice during cooking.

6 Spoon the mixture around the chicken and serve sprinkled with the sliced olives.

Normandy-Style Pork Chops

Serves 4

3 tablespoons olive oil

4 pork chops, skin removed and trimmed of excess fat

1 garlic clove, crushed

1 small onion, finely chopped

1½ tablespoons plain flour

150 ml (¼ pint) medium-dry cider

4 tablespoons water

6 sage leaves, shredded

3–4 tablespoons double cream

salt and freshly ground black pepper

1 Pre-heat a large browning dish to maximum, following the manufacturer's instructions, and add the oil during the last 20 seconds.

2 Without removing the dish from the oven, place the chops in the hot oil and microwave, uncovered, on High for 8 minutes, turning the chops over and repositioning them halfway through cooking. Remove the chops from the dish and reserve.

3 Add the garlic and onion to the dish, cover and microwave on High for 3 minutes. Stir in the flour and microwave on High for 30 seconds, then gradually stir in the cider and microwave on High for 4 minutes, stirring frequently.

4 Stir in the water, return the chops to the dish, sprinkle with the sage and spoon the sauce over the chops. Cover and microwave on High for 2 minutes, or until the sauce begins to boil. Stir, then microwave on Low for 20 minutes, or until the chops are tender.

5 Add the cream and season with salt and pepper. Leave to stand for 5 minutes before serving.

Broccoli and Cauliflower with Garlic and Lemon

Serves 4-6

350 g (12 oz) broccoli

350 g (12 oz) white *or* green cauliflower

3 tablespoons extra-virgin olive oil *or* olive oil

1 onion, halved and thinly sliced

2 garlic cloves, crushed

2 sprigs of thyme

150 ml (¼ pint) vegetable *or* chicken stock

finely grated rind and juice of 1 lemon

salt and freshly ground black pepper

toasted pine nuts, to garnish (optional)

1 Trim the ends of the stalks of the broccoli, cut off the florets and divide into small florets. Cut the stalks diagonally into 5-mm (¼-in) thick slices.

2 Cut the cauliflower florets from the head and divide them into small florets.

3 Place the oil, onion, garlic and thyme into a casserole or ovenproof bowl and mix until well coated in oil. Cover and microwave on High for 5 minutes, stirring once halfway through cooking.

4 Add the prepared broccoli, cauliflower and the stock and mix well. Cover and microwave on High for 6 minutes, turning and repositioning the broccoli and cauliflower halfway through the cooking time.

5 Sprinkle the lemon rind and juice over the vegetables and season with salt and pepper to taste. Cover and microwave for a further 1-2 minutes or until vegetables are tender-crisp.

6 Transfer to a hot serving dish, discard the thyme and sprinkle with toasted pine nuts, if using.

Dressings, Sauces and Marinades

Vinaigrette

Makes about 150 ml (¹/₄ pint)

6 tablespoons extra-virgin olive oil *or* olive oil

2 tablespoons white wine vinegar *or* malt vinegar

¼ teaspoon caster sugar

1 teaspoon Dijon mustard

salt and freshly ground black pepper

1 Place all the ingredients in a screw-topped jar and shake vigorously until well blended.

2 Before serving, shake well once again. The prepared vinaigrette can be stored for up to 1 week before serving.

Variations

Garlic Dressing Add 1 small, halved garlic clove to the above ingredients and leave to stand for at least 1 hour, then discard the garlic before serving.

Lemon Dressing Make as for Vinaigrette, but use 1½ tablespoons lemon juice instead of the vinegar and add the finely grated rind of 1 small lemon.

Herb Dressing Whisk 1–2 tablespoons finely chopped fresh herbs of your choice into the Vinaigrette just before serving.

Shallot Dressing Add 1–2 finely chopped shallots to the Vinaigrette and leave to stand for at least 1 hour before serving.

Mayonnaise

Makes about 450 ml (¾ pint)

2 (size 2) egg yolks

½ teaspoon caster sugar (optional)

½ teaspoon Dijon mustard (optional)

salt and freshly ground black pepper

1–2 tablespoons lemon juice *or* white wine vinegar *or* use a flavoured vinegar, such as tarragon *or* garlic)

about 300 ml (½ pint) extra-virgin olive oil or olive oil

1 tablespoon hot water

1 Place the egg yolks in a clean, dry bowl, discarding the thread or any egg white.

2 Add the sugar and mustard, if using, and season with a little salt and pepper to taste and blend well with a wooden spoon or balloon whisk. Gradually blend in the lemon juice or vinegar.

3 Stand the bowl on a wetted teatowel well wrung out to keep it steady and start adding the oil, drop by drop, beating well after each addition until about a quarter of the oil has been blended in. Then, gradually increase the amount of oil added until it is being poured in a thin stream, taking care to beat thoroughly throughout.

4 When the mixture is a good, thick consistency, stir in the hot water and adjust the seasoning, if necessary (if a thinner consistency is required, add a little more hot water, or a little single cream or dry white wine, as preferred).

Note: If the mayonnaise should start to curdle, place another egg yolk in a clean bowl and gradually beat the curdled mixture into it, beating or whisking all the time – it will become smooth again.

Variations

Aïoli (Garlic Mayonnaise) Peel and crush 4–5 garlic cloves with a little salt and mix into the prepared Mayonnaise.

Tartare Sauce To the prepared Mayonnaise, add 2 tablespoons chopped capers, 2 tablespoons chopped gherkins, 1 tablespoon chopped fresh chives and 2 tablespoons double cream and mix well.

Anchovy Mayonnaise Mix 1½ tablespoons anchovy essence into the prepared Mayonnaise.

Watercress Mayonnaise Trim the stalks and blanch 1 bunch watercress leaves in boiling water for 1 minute. Drain well, rinse with cold water and drain again, then squeeze dry in kitchen paper. Purée with the prepared Mayonnaise and adjust the seasoning to taste.

Tangy Mayonnaise Add the finely grated rind of 1 orange or lemon, 1 tablespoon tomato purée and a few drops of Tabasco sauce to taste to 1 quantity Mayonnaise and mix well.

Avocado Dressing

Makes about 300 ml (½ pint)

This is quite delicious, and is best eaten the day it is made.

1 large, ripe avocado

150 ml (¼ pint) prepared Mayonnaise (see page 114)

1 tablespoon lime juice

1 tablespoon vinegar

2 tablespoons chopped fresh chives

1 small, fresh, green chilli, de-seeded and finely chopped

2 spring onions, very finely chopped

salt and freshly ground black pepper

a little single cream, if necessary

1 Cut the avocado in half, remove the stone and scoop the flesh into a blender or food processor. Add the remaining ingredients, except the salt and pepper and cream.

2 Process the mixture until smooth and turn into a bowl. Season with salt and pepper to taste and thin the consistency, if wished, with a little single cream. Serve chilled.

Sweet Mustard Dressing

Makes just over 300 ml (½ pint)

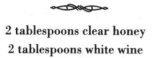

A deliciously piquant dressing – ideal for serving with chicken or pasta salads.

2 tablespoons clear honey

2 tablespoons white wine vinegar

1 tablespoon balsamic vinegar

1½ tablespoons wholegrain mustard

200 ml (⅓ pint) olive oil

salt

1 Place all the ingredients in a screw-topped jar and shake vigorously until well blended. Taste and adjust the seasoning, if necessary.

Roquefort Cheese Dressing

Makes just over 300 ml (½ pint)

Serve this with crisp green salads or wedges of iceberg lettuce.

3 tablespoons white wine *or* cider vinegar

25 g (1 oz) Roquefort cheese

3 tablespoons single cream

175 ml (6 fl oz) olive oil

salt and freshly ground black pepper

1 shallot, peeled

1 tablespoon chopped fresh chives, for sprinkling

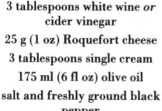

1 Place all the ingredients, except the chives, in a blender or food processor and process until smooth and blended.

2 Stir in the chopped chives.

Toasted Sesame Seed Dressing

Makes 200 ml (⅓ pint)

An unusual dressing that's good with sliced tomatoes and cheese or with fruited salads.

1½ tablespoons sesame seeds

150 ml (¼ pint) olive oil

1½ tablespoons lemon juice

1½ tablespoons malt vinegar

1 teaspoon clear honey

pinch or two of freshly grated nutmeg

pinch or two of mustard powder

½ small garlic clove, crushed

1 Toast the sesame seeds under the grill until pale golden. Leave to cool.

2 Place the remaining ingredients in a screw-topped jar and shake vigorously until well blended.

3 Just before serving, add the sesame seeds and shake vigorously once again until well blended.

Classic Basil Pesto

Makes about 300 ml (½ pint)

It is essential to use fresh basil for this wonderful dressing.

50 g (2 oz) fresh basil leaves

2 tablespoons pine nuts

100 ml (3½ fl oz) extra-virgin olive oil *or* olive oil

50 g (2 oz) Parmesan cheese, freshly grated

2 garlic cloves, peeled

salt and freshly ground black pepper

1 Place all the ingredients in a blender or food processor and process until the mixture forms a fine, creamy paste. Taste and adjust the seasoning as required.

2 Use as required. It will keep in a covered jar in the fridge for up to two weeks.

Variation

Parsley Pesto Place 25 g (1 oz) fresh sprigs of parsley and 8 fresh basil leaves in a blender or food processor. Add 100 ml (3½ fl oz) extra-virgin olive oil or olive oil, 25 g (1 oz) freshly grated Parmesan cheese, 2 tablespoons pine nuts (or use walnut pieces), 1–2 peeled garlic cloves and salt and pepper to taste. Process until the mixture forms a fine, creamy paste. Use as required and store as for Classic Basil Pesto.

Rouille

Makes about 200 ml (¹/₃ pint)

This red pepper sauce may be made with tinned pimentos, as here, or with a large, fresh red pepper (which has first been grilled, skinned, de-seeded and chopped). Rouille is a classic Provençal sauce for serving with fish, but it also goes extremely well with pasta dishes and makes a wickedly good dip for vegetables.

2 garlic cloves, peeled

2 tinned pimentos, finely chopped

3 tablespoons fresh, white breadcrumbs

1 egg yolk

1 tablespoon lemon juice

1 dried red chilli, de-seeded and finely chopped

100 ml (3½ fl oz) extra-virgin olive oil *or* olive oil

salt and freshly ground black pepper

1 Place the garlic, pimentos, breadcrumbs, egg yolk, lemon juice and chilli in a blender or food processor and process until the mixture forms a smooth paste.

2 With the machine running, gradually add the oil, drop by drop at first, and then in a thin, steady stream until the mixture thickens to resemble a rust-coloured mayonnaise.

3 Taste and adjust the seasoning as necessary.

Toasted Walnut and Chilli Dressing

Makes about 450 ml (³/₄ pint)

An interesting dressing for spooning over egg or potato salads. Good, too, as a dressing for coleslaw.

175 ml (6 fl oz) extra-virgin olive oil *or* olive oil

2 tablespoons vinegar

2 tablespoons sweet chilli sauce

1 tablespoon soft brown sugar

1 garlic clove, crushed

1 tablespoon chopped fresh parsley

150 ml (¼ pint) Mayonnaise (see page 114)

salt and freshly ground pepper

25 g (1 oz) toasted walnuts, chopped

1 Place all the ingredients, except the Mayonnaise, seasoning and walnuts, in a screw-topped jar and shake vigorously until blended.

2 Whisk the blended mixture into the Mayonnaise and adjust the seasoning, if necessary.

3 Stir in the walnuts just before serving.

Lime and Lemon Cream Dressing

Makes just over 300 ml (¹/₂ pint)

Use this instead of mayonnaise. It is especially good with prawns and other seafood, or serve as a tasty dip for crudités.

2 teaspoons sugar

finely grated rind and juice of ¹/₂ a lemon

finely grated rind and juice of 1 lime

6 tablespoons olive oil

150 ml (¹/₄ pint) double cream

few drops of Tabasco sauce, to taste

2 shallots, finely chopped

salt and freshly ground black pepper

1 Place the sugar, lemon and lime rinds and juices into a bowl. Add the oil and whisk well.

2 Gradually whisk in the cream and Tabasco, then stir in the shallots and season with salt and pepper to taste.

Spiced Wine Marinade

Makes about 300 ml (½ pint)

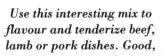

Use this interesting mix to flavour and tenderize beef, lamb or pork dishes. Good, too, for marinating chops and steaks for barbecuing.

150 ml (¼ pint) olive oil

1 teaspoon cumin seeds

1 teaspoon coriander seeds

1–2 garlic cloves, crushed

½ teaspoon chopped, dried, red chilli *or* chilli flakes

1 small onion, chopped

1 tablespoon soft brown sugar

5 tablespoons red wine

1. Heat 2 tablespoons oil in a small pan, add the cumin and coriander seeds and fry very gently for 30 seconds, stirring all the time. Remove from the heat.

2 Combine the remaining ingredients and stir in the fried spice mixture. Pour into a shallow glass dish and use as required.

Pernod Marinade

Makes about 300 ml (½ pint)

Pernod is excellent for marinating seafood, especially large, raw prawns and scallops.

4 tablespoons Pernod

juice of 2 limes

150 ml (¼ pint) olive oil

1 teaspoon fennel seeds

1–2 tablespoons chopped fresh coriander

1 small garlic clove, crushed (optional)

freshly ground black pepper

1–2 teaspoons clear honey

1 Whisk all the ingredients together and pour into a shallow glass dish. Use as required.

Flavoured Oils, Dried Tomatoes and Other Preserves

Goats' Cheese Marinated in Spiced Oil

Serves 6

450–600 ml (¾–1 pint) extra-virgin olive oil *or* olive oil

3 sprigs of rosemary

3 sprigs of thyme

a few sage leaves

1 tablespoon mixed coloured peppercorns, coarsely crushed

1 dried, red chilli

1 garlic clove

350-g (12-oz) log of goats' cheese, cut into 6 slices

1 Fill a large, wide-necked jar (with a tight-fitting lid) two-thirds full with the oil.

2 Add the herbs, crushed peppercorns, chilli and garlic, then add the cheese. Ensure the cheese is completely covered with the oil, adding more oil, if necessary.

3 Cover tightly and turn the jar over several times to ensure that the flavourings are evenly mixed.

4 Leave to marinate in the fridge for up to 2 weeks, turning the jar each day.

5 Leave to come to room temperature before serving.

Marinated Spiced Olives

Serves 6-8

These are simply delicious served as an appetizer with drinks or as an hors-d'oeuvre. They also make a wonderful addition to many salads. Once the olives have been used, use the flavoured oil that remains in salad dressings.

225 g (8 oz) Greek olives (with stones)

1 lime, sliced

1 dried, red chilli, chopped

2 garlic cloves, halved

3 allspice berries

1 teaspoon mustard seeds

2–3 sprigs of thyme *or* fennel

about 300 ml (½ pint) olive oil

1 Drain the olives. Make a small incision in each olive with a knife and place in a bowl.

2 Add the lime, chilli, garlic, allspice berries, mustard seeds and thyme or fennel. Mix all the ingredients together well.

3 Pack the mixture into a jar with a tight-fitting lid and add sufficient olive oil to cover. Turn the jar over several times to ensure the ingredients are thoroughly mixed.

4 Leave to marinate for at least 1 week before serving, turning the jar several times a day. These olives keep well for up to 2 months when stored in a cool place (if wished, you can remove the pieces of garlic after a week).

5 To serve, remove the olives from the oil and serve as required.

Herbed Garlic Oil

Makes 600 ml (1 pint)

Use this simple combination to make salad dressings and tasty marinades. The garlic is removed after a week to prevent it flavouring the oil too strongly.

small bunch of sprigs of fresh herbs (basil *or* mint *or* tarragon *or* rosemary or thyme or a mixture of several, if wished)
1–2 garlic cloves, halved, to taste
600 ml (1 pint) extra-virgin olive oil *or* olive oil

1 Lightly bruise the herb or herbs and place them in a jar or bottle with the halved garlic cloves.

2 Add the oil to fill the bottle and cover tightly.

3 Leave to marinate for 1 week, then discard the halved garlic cloves. Re-cover and continue marinating the herbs in the oil for a further 2 weeks.

4 Strain and pour the oil into a fresh bottle. Add a fresh sprig of your chosen herb or herbs (the same type or types as were used in the marinating). Re-cover and use as required.

Paprika Oil

Makes 600 ml (1 pint)

A most useful oil for cooking as it gives both colour and flavour to dishes.

600 ml (1 pint) olive oil
3 garlic cloves, halved
6 tablespoons paprika pepper

1 Heat 150 ml (¼ pint) oil in a small frying pan. Add the garlic and fry very gently for 3 minutes. Remove the pan from the heat and leave to cool, then discard the garlic.

2 Place the paprika in a bowl and gradually mix in the garlic-flavoured oil and the remaining olive oil, stirring to mix.

3 Pour the oil into a bottle, cover tightly and store in a cool, dark place. Use as required.

Preserved Lemons and Limes

Makes enough to fill a 900 g (2 lb) jar

Useful for adding zing to lots of Mediterranean dishes. Try a few slices in a marinade or add to pot-roasts, casseroles or fish stews or thread them on to skewers for barbecuing – they are especially good with seafood, chicken and pork. Do not discard the oil, it can be added to salad dressings and sauces or used to baste roasted and grilled foods.

4 lemons, scrubbed

4 limes, scrubbed

1–2 tablespoons salt

dried chilli flakes, for sprinkling *or* chopped, dried chillies, to taste

extra-virgin olive oil *or* olive oil, as required

1 Slice the lemons and limes fairly thickly and spread out in a single layer in a large dish.

2 Sprinkle with the salt and place a wedge under one end of the dish so that the liquid rendered from the fruits runs down to one side. Leave until the fruit slices become limp.

3 Remove the pips from the slices and drain the fruit in a sieve.

4 Arrange the slices in layers in the jar, sprinkling every second or third layer with a pinch or 2 of chilli flakes.

5 Press down lightly and fill the jar with sufficient olive oil to cover the top layer. Cover tightly and leave for 3–4 weeks before using as required.

Pickled Mushrooms in Oil

Serves 6

Delicious served with cold meats or cheeses or as an hors-d'oeuvre.

450 g (1 lb) button mushrooms, wiped

150 ml (¼ pint) white wine vinegar *or* light malt vinegar

½ teaspoon pickling spice

½ garlic clove, crushed

1 strip of lemon peel

1 sprig of thyme

1 sprig of rosemary

pinch of dried oregano

450–600 ml (¾–1 pint) olive oil

salt and freshly ground black pepper

1 Trim the mushrooms, if necessary. Place the vinegar, pickling spice, garlic, lemon peel and herbs in a stainless steel saucepan. Add 5 tablespoons of the oil and salt and pepper to taste.

2 Bring the mixture to the boil and add a quarter of the mushrooms. Cover and cook for 3–4 minutes, or until the mushrooms are just cooked.

3 Using a draining spoon, remove the mushrooms to a nylon sieve standing over a bowl and drain, reserving any liquid. Cook the remaining mushrooms in the same way, reserving any liquid as before.

4 Place the mushrooms in a wide-necked jar. Add the reserved liquid to the liquid left in the saucepan and boil vigorously for 3 minutes.

5 Leave to cool slightly, then pour over the mushrooms. Leave to cool completely, then add sufficient oil to cover the contents by about 2.5 cm (1 in).

6 Store the jar in the fridge and use as required, but always ensure the mushrooms are covered with a thick layer of oil. They will keep for 3 months.

Dried Tomatoes in Olive Oil

Makes 900 g–1.1 kg (2–2½ lb)

Sun-dried tomatoes are rather expensive, so why not dry your own instead? After all, the method is a simple one. If wished, add a few sprigs of fresh basil, oregano or marjoram to the jars of tomatoes before covering them with the oil. Once you have used the tomatoes, the flavoured oil makes a most useful ingredient for marinades, basting, salad dressings and sautéing.

450 g (1 lb) small, even-sized tomatoes, halved

a few sprigs of fresh basil *or* oregano *or* marjoram (optional)

1 garlic clove, halved (optional)

about 450–600 ml (¾–1 pint) olive oil

1 Pre-heat the oven to 110°C (225°F) Gas mark ¼. Grease a baking sheet.

2 Arrange the tomatoes, cut sides up, on the prepared baking sheet.

3 Place in the pre-heated oven for 2–3 hours, or until the tomatoes are dried out and shrivelled.

4 Leave to cool, then place the tomatoes in small (250-ml/8-fl oz) jars, with a few sprigs of herbs and the halved garlic clove, if using, and add sufficient oil to cover.

5 Cover tightly and store for at least 1 month before using. Once opened, store in the refrigerator and use within 2 weeks.

Pepperoni
Serves 6-8

This wonderful Italian salad of roasted and skinned sweet peppers is steeped in a delicious blend of seasonings and olive oil. Enjoy it simply with crusty bread as a starter, as part of an antipasto or as a tasty accompaniment to a main dish.

3 red peppers

3 yellow peppers

2–3 garlic cloves, slivered

3 sprigs of thyme

½–1 teaspoon dried oregano

1 dried, red chilli (optional)

1 teaspoon mixed coloured peppercorns, coarsely crushed

150 ml (¼ pint) wine vinegar *or* sherry vinegar

600 ml (1 pint) olive oil, or as required

1 Place the peppers under a hot grill until the skins blister and blacken. Place them in a sealed polythene bag and leave until cool enough to handle. Peel off the skins, discarding the stalk ends and seeds and cut the peppers into fairly thick slices.

2 Place the pepper slices in a large, wide-necked jar (with a tight-fitting lid). Add the garlic, thyme, oregano, chilli, if using, peppercorns and vinegar.

3 Add sufficient oil to cover the peppers completely. Cover and turn the jar upside-down a few times to blend the ingredients well together.

4 Store in a cool, dark place for at least 2 weeks before serving.

5 Once opened, store the jar in the fridge and ensure the contents always remain covered with oil. The peppers keep for 3 months but use within 2 weeks once opened.

Breads

Olive Oil Rolls with Sun-Dried Tomatoes

Makes 12 rolls

50 g (2 oz) sun-dried tomatoes in oil, drained and chopped

200 ml (⅓ pint) boiling water

450 g (1 lb) strong white flour

½ teaspoon salt

1 tablespoon sugar

1 sachet easy-blend yeast

1 teaspoon dried oregano *or* mixed herbs

5 tablespoons extra-virgin olive oil *or* olive oil, plus extra for greasing

1 egg, beaten

1 Put the tomatoes into a bowl with the boiling water and leave to soak for 10 minutes.

2 Sift the flour and salt into a bowl, add the sugar, yeast and oregano or mixed herbs. Mix well and make a well in the centre. Add the oil to the well, together with the tomatoes and water. Reserve 1 tablespoon beaten egg for glazing and add the remainder to the flour mixture. Mix well to form a dough.

3 Knead the dough (preferably by hand, to prevent breaking up the tomatoes) until smooth and elastic. Divide into 12 portions and shape into rolls (knots, flat Focaccia-style cakes or rounds, as wished).

4 Place on greased baking sheets, cover with lightly oiled polythene and leave in a warm place to rise until doubled in size (about 1 hour).

5 Meanwhile, pre-heat the oven to 200°C (400°F) Gas mark 6.

6 Brush the rolls lightly with the reserved egg. Bake in the oven for 12 minutes or until they are golden and sound hollow when tapped on the bases. Serve warm or cold.

Spanish Seeded Cornbread

Makes 1 large loaf

175 g (6 oz) cornmeal
¼ teaspoon salt
350 ml (12 fl oz) boiling water
3 tablespoons extra-virgin olive oil, plus extra for greasing
400 g (14 oz) strong white flour
1 sachet easy-blend yeast
milk, to glaze
1½ tablespoons sesame seeds

1 Place the cornmeal and salt in a bowl and make a well in the centre. Add the boiling water and the oil to the well and mix together with a fork until loosely blended.

2 Mix the flour with the yeast and stir into the cornmeal mixture to form a soft dough.

3 Knead the dough on a floured surface until smooth (do not add more liquid – the dough softens and becomes more pliable during kneading).

4 Shape the dough into a ball and roll out to a 23-cm (9-in) diameter round. Place on a large, greased baking sheet and make a cut 2.5 cm (1 in) in from the edge, right through to the base, all the way round. Brush with milk and sprinkle with sesame seeds.

5 Cover with lightly oiled polythene and leave to rise in a warm place for about 1 hour, or until doubled in size. Towards the end of this time, pre-heat the oven to 200°C (400°F) Gas mark 6.

6 Bake the cornbread in the pre-heated oven for about 20 minutes, or until golden brown and cooked through. Serve warm or cold.

Focaccia

Makes 1 large loaf

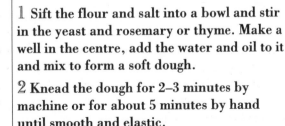

450 g (1 lb) strong white flour

¼ teaspoon salt

1 sachet easy-blend yeast

1 teaspoon chopped fresh
rosemary *or* thyme

300 ml (½ pint) hand-hot water

3 tablespoons extra-virgin
olive oil *or* olive oil, plus extra
for greasing

75 g (3 oz) pitted green olives

water, for brushing

coarse sea salt, for sprinkling

1 Sift the flour and salt into a bowl and stir in the yeast and rosemary or thyme. Make a well in the centre, add the water and oil to it and mix to form a soft dough.

2 Knead the dough for 2–3 minutes by machine or for about 5 minutes by hand until smooth and elastic.

3 Place the dough on a large, greased baking sheet. Press into a round about 25 cm (10 in) in diameter. Press the olives into the dough. Cover with lightly oiled polythene and leave in a warm place for about 30 minutes, or until doubled in size. Pre-heat the oven to 200°C (400°F) Gas mark 6.

4 Brush the dough with water and sprinkle with coarse salt. Bake in the pre-heated oven for 15–20 minutes, or until lightly golden and cooked through. Serve warm or cold.

Walnut and Onion Bread
Makes 1 loaf

1 onion

5 tablespoons extra-virgin olive oil *or* olive oil

5 tablespoons hand-hot water

100 ml (3½ fl oz) milk

1 egg, beaten

450 g (1 lb) strong white flour

½ teaspoon salt

100 g (4 oz) walnut pieces

1 sachet easy-blend yeast

1 Chop half the onion fairly finely and thinly slice the remainder. Heat 4 tablespoons oil in a frying pan, add the chopped onion and cook very gently for 5 minutes.

2 Remove from the heat and cool slightly, then add the water and milk to the pan. Reserve 1 tablespoon beaten egg for glazing and add the remainder to the onion mixture in the pan.

3 Sift the flour and salt into a bowl, stir in the walnuts and yeast and make a well in the centre. Add the oil and onion mixture to the well and mix to form a dough.

4 Knead the dough (preferably by hand to avoid breaking up the walnuts) for about 5 minutes until smooth and elastic. Form the dough into a 28-cm (11-in) long roll and place on a greased baking sheet. Cover with lightly oiled polythene and leave to rise in a warm place for about 1 hour, or until doubled in size.

5 Pre-heat the oven to 200°C (400°F) Gas mark 6.

6 Using a sharp knife, slash the top of the loaf several times crossways and then twice lengthways. Bake in the pre-heated oven for 15 minutes, then reduce the temperature to 190°C (375°F) Gas mark 5.

7 Brush the loaf with the reserved beaten egg and scatter with the sliced onions. Drizzle with the remaining oil and continue cooking for a further 15–20 minutes, or until golden and cooked through (the loaf should sound hollow when tapped on the base).

Pizza Giorgio
Makes 2 x 30-cm (12-in) round pizzas

For the pizza dough

450 g (1 lb) strong white flour

½ teaspoon salt

1 sachet easy-blend yeast

300 ml (½ pint) hand-hot water

3 tablespoons extra-virgin
olive oil *or* olive oil

For the topping

7 tablespoons extra-virgin
olive oil *or* olive oil

1 onion, chopped

2 garlic cloves, crushed

400-g (14-oz) tin chopped
tomatoes

3 tablespoons tomato purée

salt and freshly ground black
pepper

1 teaspoon chopped fresh
oregano *or* marjoram

175 g (6 oz) peperoni sausage,
skinned and sliced

175 g (6 oz) mushrooms, sliced

1–2 tablespoons chillies,
pickled in sweetened vinegar
(optional)

225 g (8 oz) Mozzarella cheese,
chopped

oregano leaves, for sprinkling

1 First, prepare the topping. Heat
6 tablespoons oil in a pan, add the onion,
garlic, tomatoes, tomato purée, salt and
pepper to taste and oregano or marjoram.
Simmer gently, uncovered, for about
6 minutes until thick. Remove from the heat
and leave to cool.

2 To make the pizza dough, put the flour,
salt and yeast in a bowl and mix together.
Make a well in the centre, add the water and
oil to it and mix well to form a dough.

3 Knead the dough for 2–3 minutes by
machine or for about 5 minutes by hand
until smooth and elastic. Divide the dough in
half and roll out each piece to form a 30-cm
(12-in) diameter pizza base. Either line
2 pizza plates with the dough or place them
on two baking sheets.

4 Spread the cooled tomato mixture over
each base to within 1 cm (½ in) of the edges.
Arrange the peperoni, mushrooms and
chillies, if using, on top. Sprinkle with the
chopped cheese and drizzle with the
remaining oil.

5 Leave in a warm place until the dough rises
slightly around the edges and looks puffy
(about 20–30 minutes) and pre-heat the oven
to 200°C (400°F) Gas mark 6.

6 Bake the pizzas for 20–25 minutes,
changing positions in the oven halfway
through cooking, until golden and cooked
through. Sprinkle with oregano leaves just
before serving.

Hot Ham, Cheese and Garlic Baguettes

Serves 4

150 ml (¼ pint) extra-virgin olive oil *or* olive oil

2 garlic cloves, crushed

1 onion, chopped

2 baguettes

2 tablespoons Dijon mustard *or* tomato relish

175 g (6 oz) sliced ham

225 g (8 oz) Mozzarella or Gruyère cheese, sliced

freshly ground black pepper

1 Pre-heat the oven to 190°C (375°F) Gas mark 5.

2 Heat 4 tablespoons oil in a frying pan. Add the garlic and onion and fry gently for 5 minutes. Remove the pan from the heat and mix in 2 tablespoons oil.

3 Cut the baguettes in half lengthways. Dip the cut sides into the oil mixture and place, crust sides down, in a shallow baking dish (a piece of crumpled foil placed in the dish prevents the bread tipping over).

4 Top the baguettes with the garlic and onion mixture and spread with the mustard or relish. Arrange the slices of ham on top (folded to fit the bread) and cover with the sliced cheese. Sprinkle with pepper to taste and brush the sides of the bread with oil and drizzle the remaining oil over the surface.

5 Cover with greased foil and bake in the pre-heated oven for 10 minutes. Remove the foil and continue cooking for a further 8–10 minutes until the topping has melted and is bubbling. Serve at once.

Pan Bagna

Serves 4

---

1 baguette

6 tablespoons extra-virgin
olive oil *or* olive oil

1 garlic clove, crushed

2 tablespoons lemon juice

1 teaspoon wholegrain mustard

½ teaspoon sugar

salt and freshly ground black
pepper

8 crisp lettuce leaves

4 tomatoes, sliced

185-g (6-oz) tin pimentos,
drained and sliced

2 small green peppers, de-
seeded and sliced into rings

16 pitted black olives, sliced

50-g (2-oz) tin anchovy fillets,
drained and coarsely chopped

---

1 Cut the baguette into 4 pieces and slice
each piece in half lengthways. Pull out most
of the soft bread from the inside.

2 Whisk the oil with the garlic, lemon juice,
mustard and sugar, and season with salt and
pepper to taste.

3 Brush a little of the garlic-flavoured
dressing over the insides of the bread.
Arrange half the lettuce on the bottom half of
each piece of bread and cover with slices of
tomato and pimento. Top each with rings of
green pepper and sprinkle with the sliced
olives and chopped anchovies.

4 Sprinkle generously with the remaining
dressing, then add the lettuce leaves and
cover with the top pieces of bread.

5 Place the filled breads on a plate, cover
with a board and weigh down with heavy
weights. Chill for at least 2 hours before
serving.

Fruit and Spice Pizza Pie
Serves 6

For the filling and topping

225 g (8 oz) seedless red grapes

3 tablespoons strawberry, raspberry *or* blackcurrant jam

½ cooking apple, peeled, cored and chopped

25 g (1 oz) soft brown sugar

¼ teaspoon ground cinnamon

¼ teaspoon ground allspice

beaten egg, to glaze

25 g (1 oz) blanched, flaked almonds

whipped cream *or* fromage frais *or* ice-cream, to serve

For the pizza dough

225 g (8 oz) strong white flour

¼ teaspoon salt

1 teaspoon soft brown sugar

½ sachet easy-blend yeast

6 tablespoons hand-hot water

2 tablespoons mild and light olive oil, plus extra for greasing

2 tablespoons beaten egg

1 Pre-heat the oven to 200°C (400°F) Gas mark 6. Grease a 20-cm (8-in) cake tin.

2 First, prepare the grapes for the topping. Place them in a baking dish and bake in the pre-heated oven for about 15 minutes until they are soft and the skins have wrinkled. Remove from the oven and leave to cool (leave the oven on).

3 Next, prepare the pizza dough. Sift the flour and salt into a bowl, add the sugar and yeast and mix well. Make a well in the centre, add the water, oil and beaten egg to the well, and mix to form a dough.

4 Knead the dough for 2–3 minutes by machine or for about 5 minutes by hand until smooth and elastic. Divide the dough in half and roll each piece to make a 20-cm (8-in) diameter round.

5 Place one round of dough in the prepared tin and spread the jam to within 1 cm (½ in) of the edges. Spoon the grapes and apple on top. Mix the sugar with the cinnamon and allspice and sprinkle half of the mixture over the fruits. Dampen the dough around the edges.

6 Place the second round of dough on top and press firmly around the edges to seal. Brush with beaten egg to glaze and make a small hole in the centre. Sprinkle with the almonds and the remaining sugar and spice mixture.

7 Cover with lightly oiled polythene and leave for about 45 minutes to rise until doubled in size. Bake in the oven for 10 minutes until golden, then cover with foil, reduce the oven temperature to 190°C (375°F) Gas mark 5 and continue cooking for a further 15 minutes, or until cooked through. Serve warm with cream, fromage frais or ice-cream.

Greek Raisin Roll

Makes 1 loaf

400 g (14 oz) strong white flour

pinch of salt

50 g (2 oz) caster sugar

½ sachet easy-blend yeast

1 egg, beaten

100 ml (3½ fl oz) tepid milk

3 tablespoons tepid water

3 tablespoons mild and light olive oil, plus extra for greasing

20 g (¾ oz) butter, melted

225 g (8 oz) seedless raisins

50 g (2 oz) walnuts *or* almonds, toasted *or* hazelnuts, chopped

1 teaspoon ground cinnamon

2 tablespoons soft brown sugar

icing sugar, for dusting

1 Place 225 g (8 oz) flour in a bowl, stir in the salt, sugar and yeast and make a well in the centre. Reserve 1 teaspoon beaten egg for glazing and add the remainder to the well in the flour, together with the milk, water and 2 tablespoons oil. Mix well to form a smooth batter.

2 Cover with lightly oiled polythene and leave in a warm place for 30 minutes to rise.

3 Add the remaining flour to the batter and mix to form a dough. Turn on to a lightly floured surface and knead the dough for 2 minutes.

4 Roll the dough to form a rectangle about 23 x 33 cm (9 x 13 in). Mix the melted butter with the remaining oil, raisins, nuts, cinnamon and brown sugar, and spread over the dough to within 5 mm (¼ in) of the edges. Lightly press the fruit mixture on to the dough.

5 Roll up from one of the short sides like a Swiss roll, and place the roll on a greased baking sheet with the join underneath. Cover with lightly oiled polythene and leave to rise in a warm place for about an hour until doubled in size and pre-heat the oven to 180°C (350°F) Gas mark 4.

6 Slash the top of the roll to form a criss-cross design. Brush the roll with the reserved beaten egg and bake in the pre-heated oven for 25–30 minutes, or until golden and cooked.

7 Leave to cool and dust with icing sugar before slicing.

Note: Although this roll is especially delicious eaten freshly baked, it is also extremely good toasted and buttered a day or two after baking.

Chocolate Spice Honey Buns
Makes 8

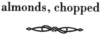

For the dough

225 g (8 oz) strong white flour

pinch of salt

1 teaspoon sugar

½ sachet easy-blend yeast

3 tablespoons mild and light olive oil, plus extra for greasing

2 tablespoons beaten egg, plus extra for glazing

6 tablespoons tepid water

For the filling and topping

25 g (1 oz) butter, softened

100 g (4 oz) soft brown sugar

1½ teaspoons ground allspice

50 g (2 oz) plain chocolate, chopped

50 g (2 oz) toasted blanched almonds, chopped

1 Grease a 23-cm (9-in) diameter cake tin and line the base with greased greaseproof paper, using 10 g (¼ oz) of the butter.

2 First, make the dough. Put the flour, salt, sugar and yeast into a bowl and make a well in the centre. Add the oil, 2 tablespoons beaten egg and the water to the well, and mix to form a dough. Knead dough on a lightly floured surface for 2–3 minutes until smooth and elastic. Roll out on a lightly floured surface to form a rectangle 36 x 23 cm (14 x 9 in).

3 Next, make the filling. Spread the remaining softened butter over the dough to within 5 mm (¼ in) of the edges.

4 Mix the brown sugar with the allspice and sprinkle half the mixture over the dough. Scatter with the chocolate and almonds and roll lightly with a rolling pin. Coat the prepared cake tin with half the remaining spiced sugar.

5 Starting from a long side, roll the dough up like a Swiss roll. Cut into 8 equal-sized slices. Put the slices in the prepared cake tin, cut sides down, and press fairly firmly with a knife to form pinwheels.

6 Brush with beaten egg to glaze and sprinkle with the remaining sugar and spice mixture.

7 Cover with lightly oiled polythene and leave to rise in a warm place for about 45 minutes until doubled in size and filling the tin. Pre-heat the oven to 180°C (350°F) Gas mark 4.

8 Bake in the pre-heated oven for 20–25 minutes, covering with foil, if necessary, during cooking to prevent the buns overbrowning. Leave to cool in the tin for 5 minutes, then turn out and remove the lining paper. Serve warm or cold.

Cakes and Puddings

Tipsy Apricot, Cherry and Nut Cake

Makes one 18-cm (7-in) cake

Enjoy this cake for afternoon tea. It has a moist, crumbly texture and a deliciously unusual flavour. Because the mixture contains lots of fruit, but no egg, it does not rise very much.

150 ml (¼ pint) mild and light olive oil, plus extra for greasing

225 g (8 oz) self-raising flour

50 g (2 oz) caster sugar

finely grated rind of ½ an orange

100 g (4 oz) no-soak apricots, chopped

100 g (4 oz) glacé cherries, quartered

25 g (1 oz) mixed nuts, chopped

100 ml (4 fl oz) milk

4 tablespoons Marsala *or* sweet sherry *or* Madeira

1–2 tablespoons demerara sugar

1 Pre-heat the oven to 180°C (350°F) Gas mark 4. Grease an 18-cm (7-in) diameter, deep cake tin and line the base with greased greaseproof paper.

2 Sift the flour into a bowl, stir in the sugar, orange rind, apricots, 50 g (2 oz) cherries and the nuts, and make a well in the centre. Add the milk and Marsala, sherry or Madeira to the well, and, using a wooden spoon, mix in as much of the flour and sugar as you can (you may find the ingredients quite difficult to mix at this stage as the mixture is rather glutinous before the oil is added).

3 Heat the 150 ml (¼ pint) oil in a small pan until warm, then pour on to the cake mixture and beat well together.

4 Spoon the mixture into the prepared tin and level the surface. Scatter the remaining cherries and demerara sugar over the surface.

5 Bake in the pre-heated oven for 45–55 minutes, or until the cake is golden and cooked through. Leave the cake to cool in the tin for 10 minutes, then turn it out on to a wire rack to cool completely before serving.

Strawberry Cream Cheesecake
Serves 8

For the sponge

65 g (2½ oz) self-raising flour

½ teaspoon baking powder

50 g (2 oz) caster sugar

3 tablespoons mild and light olive oil, plus extra for greasing

1 egg, beaten

1½ tablespoons milk

2 drops vanilla essence

For the filling

3 tablespoons orange juice

225 g (8 oz) full-fat soft cheese

50 g (2 oz) caster sugar

½ x 425-g (15-oz) tin custard

1 x 11-g (⅓-oz) sachet powdered gelatine

4 tablespoons cold water

150 ml (¼ pint) double cream

2 egg whites

For the topping and decoration

40 g (1½ oz) flaked almonds, toasted

175 g (6 oz) strawberries, hulled and halved

2 tablespoons redcurrant jelly

1 tablespoon water

1 Pre-heat the oven to 190°C (375°F) Gas mark 5. Grease an 18-cm (7-in) diameter cake tin and line the base with greased greaseproof paper.

2. First, make the sponge. Sift the flour and baking powder into a bowl and stir in the sugar. Put the oil, egg, milk and vanilla essence in a bowl and mix well. Pour into the flour mixture and stir with a wooden spoon until creamy, then beat for 1 minute.

3 Transfer the mixture to the prepared tin, level the surface and cook in the pre-heated oven for 25–30 minutes, or until well risen and golden brown. Turn on to a wire rack and leave to cool.

4 Lightly oil the sides of an 18-cm (7-in) diameter, loose-bottomed, deep cake tin and line the base and sides with greased greaseproof paper.

5 Cut the cooked sponge in half horizontally and place the top half in the tin, trimming it as necessary so it fits neatly. Sprinkle with the orange juice.

6 Now, make the rest of the filling. Place the soft cheese and sugar in a bowl and beat until smooth. Add the custard and beat until well mixed.

7 Sprinkle the gelatine over the cold water in a small, heatproof basin and leave for 5 minutes to soften. Stand the basin in a pan of simmering water and stir until the gelatine dissolves. Leave until it has cooled, but not set.

8 Stir the cooled, but runny, gelatine into the cheese and custard mixture. Whip the cream until it forms soft peaks, then whisk the egg whites until they are the same. Fold the cream

and egg whites into the cheese and custard mixture using a metal spoon.

9 Transfer the mixture to the tin and level the surface. Top with the remaining half of the sponge, placing it base side upwards, and chill for at least 4 hours until set.

10 Now, decorate the cheesecake and make the topping. Remove the cheesecake from the tin and carefully peel away the greaseproof paper. Press the almonds on to the side of the cheesecake and transfer it to a serving plate.

11 Arrange the halved strawberries, cut sides down, on the top of the cheesecake. Heat the redcurrant jelly and water together in a small pan until melted. Leave to cool, then brush over the strawberries to form a glaze.

Note: fresh raspberries would make a delicious topping variation.

Baklava

Makes about 25 portions

For the Baklava

5 tablespoons mild and light olive oil, plus extra for greasing

50 g (2 oz) caster sugar

100 g (4 oz) blanched almonds, chopped

100 g (4 oz) walnuts, chopped

1 teaspoon ground cinnamon

1 teaspoon ground allspice

90 g (3½ oz) unsalted butter, melted

450 g (1 lb) frozen filo pastry, defrosted

For the spiced syrup

325 ml (11 fl oz) cold water

350 g (12 oz) granulated sugar

1 cinnamon stick

4 whole cloves

2 strips of lemon peel

2 tablespoons Greek honey

1 Pre-heat the oven to 160°C (325°F) Gas mark 3. Grease a 25 x 33-cm (10 x 13-in) roasting tin.

2 Mix together the sugar, nuts and spices. In another bowl, mix the 5 tablespoons oil with the melted butter.

3 Line the base of the prepared tin with 1 sheet of filo pastry, trimming it to fit. Brush with the oil and butter mixture. Cover with 7 more sheets of filo pastry, trimming and brushing each one with the oil mixture (you may need to gently heat the oil mixture if it starts to thicken before you have finished).

4 Sprinkle half the nut mixture over the pastry, then cover with 4 more sheets of pastry, trimming and brushing each one with the oil mixture as before.

5 Sprinkle the remaining nut mixture on top and cover with 5 more sheets of filo pastry, trimming and brushing with oil mixture. Brush any remaining oil mixture on top.

6 Using a sharp knife, cut through the top layers of pastry to make 25 diamond-shaped pieces. Bake in the pre-heated oven for about 1 hour, or until golden brown, covering with foil, if necessary, to prevent overbrowning. Leave in the tin to cool.

7 Meanwhile, make the spiced syrup. Place all the ingredients in a large saucepan and heat gently, stirring to dissolve the sugar. Boil for 5 minutes, then strain the mixture over the baklava in the tin. Leave to soak for 8 hours or overnight before serving.

Moist Lemon Honey Sponge

Serves 9

For the sponge

150 g (5 oz) self-raising flour

1 teaspoon baking powder

120 g (4½ oz) caster sugar

6 tablespoons mild and light olive oil, plus extra for greasing

3 tablespoons milk

2 eggs

finely grated rind of 1 lemon

For the syrup

a little water

juice of 2 or 3 lemons

75 g (3 oz) granulated sugar

2 tablespoons clear honey

For the topping

thick Greek yogurt *or* fromage frais, to serve

1 Pre-heat the oven to 180°C (350°F) Gas mark 4. Grease a 20-cm (8-in) square deep cake tin and line the base and sides with greased greaseproof paper.

2 First, make the sponge. Sift the flour and baking powder into a bowl and stir in the sugar. In another bowl, mix the oil, milk, eggs and lemon rind well together. Pour into the flour mixture and stir with a wooden spoon until creamy, then beat well for 2 minutes.

3 Pour the mixture into the prepared tin and level the surface, ensuring the mixture fills the corners of the tin.

4 Bake in the pre-heated oven for 35–40 minutes, or until well risen, golden and springy to the touch. Leave to cool in the tin for 5 minutes.

5 Loosen the sponge from the tin and turn out on to a plate (the plate needs to be large and deep enough to hold the cake while soaking it in the hot syrup).

6 To make the syrup, add enough water to the lemon juice to make it up to 225 ml (8 fl oz). Pour into a saucepan and add the sugar. Stir over a low heat until the sugar dissolves. Boil for 3 minutes, then stir in the honey. Remove from the heat.

7 Prick the top of the cake with a fine skewer and spoon the hot syrup over the cake. Leave to cool completely.

8 Cut into neat portions and serve with spoonfuls of Greek yogurt or fromage frais.

Chocolate and Amaretto Gâteau
Serves 8-10

For the sponge
150 g (5 oz) plain flour
25 g (1 oz) cocoa powder
pinch of salt
2 teaspoons baking powder
150 g (5 oz) soft brown sugar
2 (size 2) eggs, separated
6 tablespoons mild and light olive oil, plus extra for greasing
6 tablespoons milk

For the Amaretto syrup
100 g (4 oz) granulated sugar
150 ml (¼ pint) water
4 tablespoons Amaretto

For the decoration
300 ml (½ pint) double cream
ratafia biscuits and chocolate caraque

1 Pre-heat the oven to 180°C (350°F) Gas mark 4. Grease a 1.4–1.7-litre (2½–3-pint) ring tin.

2 Sift the flour, cocoa, salt and baking powder into a bowl and stir in the sugar. In another bowl, mix the egg yolks with the oil and milk, then pour it into the flour mixture. Beat well until you have a smooth batter.

3 Whisk the egg whites until stiff and fold into the cake mixture using a metal spoon.

4 Pour the mixture into the prepared tin and cook in the pre-heated oven for 45–50 minutes, or until it is well risen and cooked through.

5 Turn the cake out on to a wire rack and leave to cool.

6 Meanwhile, make the Amaretto syrup. Place the sugar and water in a pan and heat slowly, stirring to dissolve the sugar. Bring to the boil and boil for 5 minutes, then remove from the heat and add the Amaretto.

7 Return the cake to the tin and prick the surface several times with a fine skewer. Pour the hot syrup over the cake and leave to soak for 2–3 hours.

8 Turn the cake out of the tin and place on a serving plate, ready to decorate. Whip the cream until it forms soft peaks and spread two-thirds of it over the cake to cover it.

9 Place the remaining cream in a piping bag fitted with a large star nozzle and decorate the gâteau with swirls of piped cream, ratafia biscuits and chocolate caraque (these are large chocolate curls, made by melting chocolate, pouring it on to a large marble

slab, letting it cool and set until nearly solid, then pushing a scraper or knife blade under the chocolate to form curls.

Note: This can also be made using brandy in place of Amaretto.

Spiced Fruit Cake

Makes one 18-cm (7-in) cake

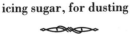

150 ml (¼ pint) mild and light olive oil, plus extra for greasing

225 g (8 oz) plain flour

2 teaspoons baking powder

pinch of salt

1 teaspoon ground mixed spice

150 g (5 oz) caster sugar

2 eggs

3–4 tablespoons milk

400 g (14 oz) mixed dried fruit

50 g (2 oz) glacé cherries, quartered

40 g (1½ oz) flaked almonds

icing sugar, for dusting

1 Pre-heat the oven to 160°C (325°F) Gas mark 3. Grease an 18-cm (7-in) diameter, deep cake tin and line the base and sides with greased greaseproof paper.

2 Sift the flour, baking powder, salt and mixed spice into a bowl and stir in the sugar. Add the oil, eggs and 3 tablespoons milk and beat thoroughly with a wooden spoon for 2 minutes.

3 Stir in the mixed fruit and cherries and a little more milk, if necessary, so the mixture is of a dropping consistency.

4 Transfer the mixture to the prepared tin. Level the surface and scatter with the almonds.

5 Bake in the pre-heated oven for 1 hour, then reduce the temperature to 150°C (300°F) Gas mark 2 and continue cooking for a further 1¼ hours or until cooked through, covering with foil, if necessary, during cooking to prevent overbrowning (test whether it is done by inserting a skewer into the centre of the cake: if it comes out clean, the cake is cooked; if not, return the cake to the oven and cook for a further few minutes before testing again).

6 Leave the cake to cool in the tin, then turn out and remove the lining paper. Store in an airtight tin for at least 1 day before cutting. Liberally dust with icing sugar before slicing and serving.

Nectarine and Crème Pâtissière Gâteau

Serves 8

For the cake

2 tablespoons mild and light olive oil, plus extra for greasing

4 eggs, separated

100 g (4 oz) caster sugar

100 g (4 oz) self-raising flour

3 tablespoons boiling water

few drops of vanilla essence

For the crème pâtissière

3 (size 2) egg yolks

50 g (2 oz) caster sugar

25 g (1 oz) plain flour

300 ml (½ pint) milk

25 g (1 oz) butter

2 teaspoons sherry

For the filling and decoration

2 tablespoons apricot jam

300 ml (½ pint) double cream

50 g (2 oz) hazelnuts, toasted and chopped

2 or 3 ripe nectarines *or* peaches

2 teaspoons lemon juice

4 tablespoons orange marmalade without shreds

1 Pre-heat the oven to 180°C (350°F) Gas mark 4. Grease a 20-cm (8-in) diameter, loose-bottomed, deep cake tin and line the base and sides with greased greaseproof paper.

2 Place the egg yolks, sugar, flour, 2 tablespoons oil, water and vanilla essence in a bowl and beat well for 2 minutes.

3 Whisk the egg whites until stiff and fold into the batter using a metal spoon. Pour the mixture into the prepared tin and bake in the pre-heated oven for 50–60 minutes, or until well risen and cooked through.

4 Carefully remove from the tin and leave to cool on a wire rack. Remove the lining paper once the cake is cold.

5 To make the crème pâtissière, place the egg yolks and sugar in a bowl and beat until smooth and creamy. Stir in the flour and mix well. Heat the milk until hot, but not boiling, and gradually stir into the egg mixture. Rinse out the pan, return the mixture to it and bring to the boil over a low heat, stirring all the time. Cook for 2–3 minutes, stirring. Remove from the heat and beat in the butter and sherry.

6 Pour the mixture into a bowl and leave to cool, covered closely with dampened greaseproof paper to prevent a skin forming.

7 Cut the cold cake into 3 layers. Place the bottom layer on a serving plate and spread with 1 tablespoon apricot jam and half the cold crème pâtissière. Place the second layer of cake on top and spread with the remaining apricot jam and crème pâtissière. Top with the third layer of cake.

8 Whip the cream until it forms soft peaks and spread half of it on the top and around the sides of the cake. Coat the sides with the hazelnuts.

9 Slice the nectarines (or peel and slice the peaches) and arrange on top of the cake in a 'wheel' pattern. Brush lightly with lemon juice.

10 Heat the marmalade in a small pan until it is runny and, while it is still warm, brush it over the nectarines or peaches.

11 Place the remaining whipped cream in a piping bag fitted with a medium star nozzle and use it to decorate the gâteau.

Fruit and Nut Bars

Makes 18

150 ml (¼ pint) mild and light olive oil, plus extra for greasing

100 g (4 oz) self-raising flour

100 g (4 oz) rolled oats

100 g (4 oz) golden syrup

100 g (4 oz) soft brown sugar

4 tablespoons milk

1 egg, beaten

1 crisp, sharp-flavoured eating apple, peeled, cored and grated

100 g (4 oz) no-soak apricots, chopped

50 g (2 oz) flaked almonds

1 Pre-heat the oven to 160°C (325°F) Gas mark 3. Grease a 28 x 23-cm (11 x 9-in) baking tin and line the base with greased greaseproof paper.

2 Place the flour and oats in a bowl and make a well in the centre.

3 Put the syrup, sugar and 150 ml (¼ pint) oil in a saucepan and heat gently to melt the syrup and dissolve the sugar.

4 Add the syrupy mixture, milk and egg to the well in the flour mixture, and mix well. Stir in the apple, apricots and 25 g (1 oz) almonds.

5 Transfer the mixture to the prepared tin, level the surface and sprinkle with the remaining almonds.

6 Bake in the pre-heated oven for 1–1¼ hours until golden brown and cooked through. Cover with foil, if necessary, during cooking.

7 Leave it to cool before cutting into 18 bars. These keep well for up to 2 weeks, stored in an airtight container.

Apple Frangipane Tart

Serves 6

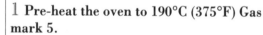

For the pastry

5 tablespoons mild and light olive oil

4½ tablespoons cold water

225 g (8 oz) plain flour

pinch of salt

For the filling

75 g (3 oz) butter

75 g (3 oz) caster sugar

1 egg, beaten

75 g (3 oz) ground almonds

20 g (¾ oz) plain flour

4 teaspoons lemon juice

3 eating apples

2 tablespoons pine nuts

For the glaze

1 tablespoon caster sugar

3 tablespoons apricot jam, sieved

1 teaspoon lemon juice

1 Pre-heat the oven to 190°C (375°F) Gas mark 5.

2 To make the pastry, using a fork, whisk the oil and water together in a bowl until evenly blended. Sift the flour and salt together in another bowl and gradually add to the oil, mixing until the ingredients form a dough.

3 Knead the pastry lightly but quickly until smooth and shiny. Roll out on a lightly floured surface to form a round large enough to line a 23-cm (9-in) loose-bottomed fluted flan tin.

4 Press the pastry firmly into the flutes and trim the top edge neatly. Prick the base all over with a fork and line with foil and baking beans.

5 Place on a baking sheet and bake in the pre-heated oven for 10 minutes. Remove the foil and beans and cook for a further 5 minutes. Place a baking sheet in the oven to heat, leaving the oven on.

6 To make the filling, cream together the butter and sugar, then beat in the egg. Fold in the ground almonds, sift in the flour and 2 teaspoons lemon juice. Spoon the mixture into the prepared flan case and spread evenly.

7 Peel and halve the apples, remove the cores and brush with the remaining lemon juice. Cut the apple halves crossways into thin slices and arrange them on the almond mixture, keeping the slices of each apple half together and placing the halves, cut sides down. Press down lightly into the almond mixture until they touch the base.

8 Sprinkle the filling with pine nuts and place the flan tin on the hot baking sheet. Cook in the oven for 10 minutes, then reduce the oven

temperature to 180°C (350°F) Gas mark 4 and continue cooking for a further 15 minutes until the apples are tender and the filling is set. Sprinkle with the caster sugar and cook for a further 5 minutes.

9 Finally, complete the glaze by warming the jam with the lemon juice until runny and brush over the surface of the hot flan. Return to the oven for a further 5 minutes to set the glaze. Serve warm or cold.

Pears on Brioche

Serves 4

Use ripe dessert pears that cook quickly – hard Conference pears just will not work! Brioche loaves vary in size, so you may need more or fewer pear slices to fit accordingly. I used a rectangular loaf-shaped Brioche (sold in supermarkets) rather than the large, classic round-shaped loaf, but either will do.

4 small, ripe Comice pears

juice of 1 lemon

4 x 1-cm (½-in) thick slices Brioche loaf

4 tablespoons mild and light olive oil

caster sugar, for sprinkling

few pinches of ground allspice *or* cinnamon (optional)

1–2 tablespoons chopped walnuts

1 Pre-heat the oven to 200°C (400°F) Gas mark 6.

2 Peel, core and slice the pears into a bowl containing the lemon juice.

3 Quickly dip both sides of the slices of Brioche into the olive oil, then place in a shallow ovenproof dish. Sprinkle lightly with caster sugar and add a pinch or two of allspice, if using.

4 Arrange the pear slices on top and sprinkle with caster sugar.

5 Bake in the pre-heated oven for 20 minutes or until the bread is crisp around the outside and the pears are tender and cooked. Sprinkle with chopped walnuts and serve hot.

Crispelle (Sicilian-Style Doughnuts)

Serves 6

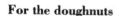

These little fried doughnuts, drizzled with spiced honey syrup, are just wonderful served hot with ice-cream.

For the doughnuts

225 g (8 oz) strong white flour

pinch of salt

25 g (1 oz) butter

1 sachet easy-blend yeast

6 tablespoons tepid milk

1 egg, beaten

mild and light olive oil, for shallow frying, plus extra for greasing

For the topping

8 tablespoons clear honey

little ground cinnamon, to taste

finely grated rind of 1 orange

1–2 tablespoons caster sugar, for sprinkling

1 Sift the flour and salt into a bowl and rub in the butter finely until the mixture resembles fine breadcrumbs. Stir in the yeast and make a well in the centre.

2 Mix the milk with the beaten egg, and add to the well in the flour mixture and mix well to form a soft dough. Mix and knead the dough on a lightly floured surface for 5-10 minutes until smooth and elastic.

3 Return the dough to the bowl, cover with lightly oiled polythene and leave to rise in a warm place for about 1 hour, or until doubled in size.

4 Knead the dough lightly and divide into 24 pieces, each about the size of a walnut, and shape into rounds. Place on a lightly oiled baking sheet and cover with lightly oiled polythene. Leave to rise in a warm place for 10 minutes.

5 Heat about 1-cm (½-in) depth of oil in a large frying pan to 180°C (350°F) or until a cube of day-old bread browns in 30 seconds. Fry the dough rounds, in batches of 6, for about 4 minutes per batch until golden brown, turning frequently. Drain on kitchen paper and keep warm while cooking the remainder in the same way.

6 Warm the honey in a small pan with the cinnamon and orange rind. Arrange the doughnuts on a serving platter and drizzle with the warmed honey mixture. Sprinkle with caster sugar and serve hot.

Mocha Pudding with Cointreau Cream

Serves 6

This sticky chocolate pudding, flavoured with strong coffee, is delicious served with alcohol-flavoured cream, but you could use fromage frais instead if you prefer.

For the pudding

50 g (2 oz) self-raising flour

25 g (1 oz) cocoa powder

6 tablespoons mild and light olive oil, plus extra for greasing

75 g (3 oz) caster sugar

finely grated rind of 1 small orange

1 (size 2) egg

For the topping

50 g (2 oz) soft brown sugar

15 g (½ oz) cocoa powder

For the sauce

300 ml (½ pint) strong, hot, black coffee

50 g (2 oz) caster sugar

For finishing

icing sugar, for dusting

150 ml (¼ pint) double cream

1 tablespoon Cointreau

1 Pre-heat the oven to 160°C (325°F) Gas mark 3. Grease a 1.2-litre (2-pint) pie dish.

2 To make the pudding, place all the pudding ingredients in a mixing bowl and beat with a wooden spoon for 2 minutes or until thoroughly mixed. Transfer the mixture to the prepared pie dish and smooth the surface. Place the dish on a baking sheet.

3 Mix the topping ingredients together and sprinkle over the surface of the pudding.

4 To make the sauce, mix the hot coffee with the caster sugar, stirring until dissolved. Pour the sweetened coffee over the pudding mixture.

5 Bake in the pre-heated oven for 50 minutes, or until the pudding is set and cooked through. Dust the pudding with sifted icing sugar.

6 Whip the cream with the Cointreau until it forms soft peaks and serve with the pudding.

Crêpes Grand Marnier
Makes 8

The perfect finale to a splendid dinner. The crêpes can be prepared in advance (to the end of step 6), ready to add the finishing touches a few minutes before they are required.

For the crêpe batter
100 g (4 oz) plain flour
pinch of salt
1 egg
1 egg yolk
250 ml (8 fl oz) milk
1 tablespoon mild and light olive oil, plus extra for cooking
2 teaspoons Grand Marnier

For the liqueur butter
8 sugar lumps
2 oranges
50 g (2 oz) unsalted butter, well softened
1 tablespoon Grand Marnier

For serving
15 g (½ oz) unsalted butter
2 tablespoons Grand Marnier
1–2 tablespoons brandy
single *or* double cream

1 First, make the crêpe batter. Sift the flour and salt into a bowl and make a well in the centre. Add the egg and egg yolk to the well and gradually stir in half the milk. Beat with a wooden spoon, gradually drawing the flour into the liquid to make a smooth batter. Stir in the remaining milk, 1 tablespoon oil and the Grand Marnier. Pour the mixture into a jug.

2 Heat a little oil in a 15–18-cm (6–7-in) frying pan, swirling it over the base and sides, and pour off any excess into a heatproof basin. Return the pan to the heat and pour in sufficient batter to coat the base of the pan thinly, tilting the pan quickly as you pour to spread the batter evenly in a thin layer.

3 Cook over a high heat for 1–1½ minutes, or until the underside is golden brown, then turn the crêpe over and cook until the other side is golden brown.

4 Transfer the crêpe to a plate and fry the remaining batter in the same way, to make 8 crêpes in total, adding more oil to the pan as necessary.

5 To make the liqueur butter, rub each lump of sugar on the skin of the oranges so they absorb the zest. Finely crush the sugar lumps and mix with the softened butter and Grand Marnier.

6 Spread the orange butter over the crêpes (the crêpes can be prepared in advance to this stage, ready to add the final touches to when required – just put the crêpes on to a plate).

7 A few minutes before serving, heat the butter in a large frying pan, add one crêpe at a time, orange-butter side down, and heat through for 30 seconds, then turn and fold in

three (making a tricorn shape) and place on a hot serving dish. Keep warm while reheating the remaining crêpes in the same way.

8 Add the Grand Marnier and brandy to the juices in the pan and heat through, ignite with a long taper or match and pour at once over the crêpes. Serve immediately with cream.

Spiced Apple Fritters

Serves 4-6

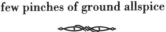

4 small eating apples

1–2 tablespoons lemon juice

100 g (4 oz) plain flour

150 ml (¼ pint) water

1 tablespoon mild and light olive oil, plus extra for shallow frying

2 egg whites

2 tablespoons caster sugar

¼ teaspoon ground cinnamon

few pinches of ground allspice

1 Core the apples, then peel and cut each one crossways into 4 slices. Brush lightly with lemon juice to prevent discoloration.

2 Sift the flour into a bowl and gradually add the water, then whisk together until the mixture is smooth and creamy. Stir in 1 tablespoon oil and mix well. Whisk the egg whites until stiff and fold into the batter using a large metal spoon.

3 Heat about 1-cm (½-in) depth of olive oil in a large frying pan to 180°C (350°F) or until a cube of day-old bread browns in 30 seconds.

4 Dip each apple ring into the batter and fry, a few at a time, for about 4 minutes, turning frequently until golden brown and cooked through. Drain on kitchen paper and keep warm while cooking the remainder in the same way.

5 Mix the caster sugar with the cinnamon and allspice and sift over the cooked fritters. Serve at once.

Glazed Fruit Tart

Serves 8-10

A pastry case holds an inviting mixture of crème pâtissière and a colourful mix of glazed fresh fruits, such as figs, strawberries, grapes, peaches and plums.

For the pastry

225 g (8 oz) plain flour

pinch of salt

1 egg, beaten

4 tablespoons mild and light olive oil

3 tablespoons water

For the filling

1 quantity crème pâtissière (see page 146)

selection of fresh fruits (say, strawberries, raspberries, blueberries, grapes, sliced figs, peaches, nectarines and plums)

150 ml (¼ pint) fromage frais

For the glaze

8 tablespoons apricot jam, sieved

1 tablespoon Kirsch

1 tablespoon water

1 First, make the pastry. Sift the flour and salt into a bowl and make a well in the centre. Add the egg, oil and water to the well and mix quickly with a fork to form a dough. Knead gently, then return to the bowl, cover with a damp cloth and leave to stand for 30 minutes. Pre-heat the oven to 190°C (375°F) Gas mark 5.

2 Roll out the pastry on a floured surface and use to line a 28-cm (11-in) loose-bottomed fluted flan tin. Press the pastry firmly into the flutes and trim the top edge neatly. Prick the base all over with a fork. Line with foil and fill with baking beans. Place on a baking sheet and cook in the pre-heated oven for 15 minutes.

3 Remove the foil and beans and cook for a further 5 minutes until the pastry is golden and cooked through. Leave to cool.

4 Meanwhile, make the crème pâtissière, as given on page 146.

5 Prepare the fruits for the tart. Mix the cold crème pâtissière with the fromage frais and use to fill the cold pastry case. Arrange the prepared fruits on top.

6 To make the glaze, gently heat the apricot jam with the Kirsch and water until the jam is runny. Brush or spoon the glaze over the fruits and leave to set before serving.

Note: This tart is best left for at least 2 hours before serving.

Variation

To make dainty, assorted fruit tartlets, use the pastry to line small barquettes (boat-shaped moulds – ideal for a party). Gently ease the

pastry into the moulds and trim neatly. Prick
the bases with a fork and line with foil and
baking beans. Place the moulds on a baking
sheet and bake at 190°C (375°F) Gas mark 5
for 6–8 minutes, or until the pastry is golden
and cooked. Leave to cool, then fill with
whipped cream, fromage frais or crème
pâtissière, and top with fresh fruits. Glaze
and leave to set before serving.

Index

A

almonds: apple frangipane
tart, 148-9
Circassian-style chicken, 56
Amaretto: chocolate and
Amaretto gâteau, 144-5
anchovies: tapenade, 11
apples: apple frangipane
tart, 148
glazed duck breasts with
apples and Calvados, 60
spiced apple fritters, 153
apricots: Moroccan lamb
with apricots, 68
tipsy apricot, cherry and
nut cake, 139
artichokes marinated with
peppers and olives, 91
asparagus, wild mushroom
and pine nut risotto, 78
aubergines: aubergine and
tomato lasagne, 80-1
aubergine and tomato
Parmigiana, 90
creamy aubergine dip, 104
monkfish in aubergine
'cannelloni' with
mushroom sauce, 38-39
Mozzarella-glazed chicken
with aubergine and
tomatoes, 51
avocados: avocado dressing,
115
avocado soup with prawn
salsa, 20
roasted mixed peppers with
avocado and olive crème
fraîche, 13
sunshine fruit and avocado
salad, 47

B

bacon: leafy salad with bacon
and brioche croûtons, 46
baklava, 142
barbecues, 93-102

basil pesto, classic, 117
beans: ribollita, 28
smoked sausage, mixed
bean and vegetable
casserole, 74
beef: individual boeuf en
croûte, 63
pasta and steak in cream
sauce, 108-9
peppered tomato steak on
brochette, 96
wine-braised beef with
porcini, 62
la bourride, 21
brandade de morue, 19
breads, 129-38
focaccia, 131
garlic croûtons, 10, 25
Greek raisin roll, 137
grilled goat's cheese on
bruschetta, 15
hot ham, cheese and garlic
baguettes, 134
olive oil rolls with sun-dried
tomatoes, 129
pan bagna, 135
Spanish seeded cornbread,
130
walnut and onion bread,
132
Brie cheese: creamed celery
soup with Brie, 106
brioche, pears en, 149
broccoli: broccoli and
cauliflower with garlic and
lemon, 112
broccoli and Roquefort
soup, 29
capellini with prawns,
broccoli and red pepper,
82
bruschetta, grilled goat's
cheese on, 15
bulgar wheat: roasted sweet
peppers with bulgar
wheat, 77

tabbouleh with scallops in a
citrus-sharp dressing, 76
buns, chocolate spice honey,
138

C

cabanos, Spanish chicken
with rice and, 59
cakes, 139-47
chocolate and Amaretto
gâteau, 144-5
fruit and nut bars, 147
moist lemon honey sponge,
143
nectarine and crème
pâtissière gâteau, 146-7
spiced fruit cake, 145
tipsy apricot, cherry and
nut cake, 139
Camembert, filo-wrapped
with watercress, 14-15
capellini with prawns,
broccoli and red pepper,
82
carrots: spiced carrot, lentil
and coriander soup, 23
cassoulet of duckling, 61
cauliflower: broccoli and
cauliflower with garlic and
lemon, 112
celery: creamed celery soup
with Brie, 106
cheese: aubergine and tomato
Parmigiana, 90
broccoli and Roquefort
soup, 29
creamed celery soup with
Brie, 106
filo-wrapped Camembert
with watercress, 14-15
fruited goats' cheese salad,
44
goats' cheese marinated in
spiced oil, 122
Greek-style cheese kebabs,
102

grilled goat's cheese on bruschetta, 15
grilled Italian-style salad, 49
hot ham, cheese and garlic baguettes, 134
leek and fennel soup with toast and cheese, 22
little Roquefort quiches, 12
Mozzarella-glazed chicken with aubergine and tomatoes, 51
Roquefort cheese dressing, 116
spanakhopitas, 17
sweet onion and Gruyère tart, 85
toasted walnut, salami and Roquefort salad, 50
veal Parmesan, 65
cheesecake, strawberry cream, 140-1
cherries: tipsy apricot, cherry and nut cake, 139
chestnuts: creamy garlic and chestnut soup, 23
chicken: barbecued chicken with red hot sauce, 98
chicken and melon salad in spiced mayonnaise, 43
Circassian-style chicken, 56
garlic lemon chicken, 54
Mediterranean chicken, 110
Mediterranean chicken pasta with garlic crumbs, 55
Moroccan-style chicken in pastry, 57
Mozzarella-glazed chicken with aubergine and tomatoes, 51
paella Valenciana, 79
Provençal chicken pepper tart, 58
Spanish chicken with rice and cabanos, 59
spiced chicken, pepper and lemon couscous, 75
spiced orange chicken with lentils, 52
wine-braised chicken rolls with herbed stuffing, 53
chickpeas: hummus, 16

pasta salad with hummus sesame dressing, 45
chilli: chillied mixed mushrooms, 86
toasted walnut and chilli dressing, 119
chocolate: chocolate and Amaretto gâteau, 144-5
chocolate spice honey buns, 138
mocha pudding with Cointreau cream, 151
Circassian-style chicken, 56
cod, salt see salt cod
coffee: mocha pudding with Cointreau cream, 151
corn cobs, pancetta-wrapped, 99
cornbread, Spanish seeded, 130
courgettes: fennel and courgettes à la Grecque, 105
couscous: lamb kibbeh with two dips, 69
spiced chicken, pepper and lemon couscous, 75
crab cakes with tomato salsa, 31
crème fraîche: peppered pork medallions with mushroom crème fraîche, 72
roasted mixed peppers with avocado and olive crème fraîche, 13
crêpes Grand Marnier, 152-3
crispelle (Sicilian-style doughnuts), 150
croûtons, garlic, 10, 25
crudités, two dips with, 16

D
dips: creamy aubergine, 104
lamb kibbeh with two dips, 69
soured cream, 100
two dips with crudités, 16
doughnuts, Sicilian-style, 150
dressings, 113-20
avocado, 115
classic basil pesto, 117
lime and lemon cream, 120

mayonnaise, 114-15
Roquefort cheese, 116
sweet mustard, 116
toasted sesame seed, 117
toasted walnut and chilli, 119
vinaigrette, 113
duck: bitter-sweet duckling salad, 41
cassoulet of duckling, 61
glazed duck breasts with apples and Calvados, 60

E
eggs tonnato on pepperoni, 48

F
fennel: fennel and courgettes à la Grecque, 105
Italian-style fennel with spinach, 84
leek and fennel soup with toast and cheese, 22
filo-wrapped Camembert with watercress, 14-15
fish, 30-40
la bourride, 21
seafood terrine with marinated prawns, 18
focaccia, 131
French beans: braised French beans and tomatoes Provençal, 89
French roast lamb with sorrel and watercress stuffing, 67
fritters, spiced apple, 153
fritto misto di mare, 37
fruit and nut bars, 147
fruit and spice pizza pie, 136
fruit cake, spiced, 145
fruit tart, glazed, 154-5
fruited goats' cheese salad, 44
fruited pork loin, 71

G
garlic: creamy garlic and chestnut soup, 23
garlic croûtons, 10, 25
garlic dip, 69
garlic lemon chicken, 54
herbed garlic oil, 124

roasted tomato and garlic soup with Parmesan, 27
gâteaux: chocolate and Amaretto, 144-5
nectarine and crème pâtissière, 146-7
gazpacho, 25
goats' cheese: fruited goats' cheese salad, 44
goats' cheese marinated in spiced oil, 122
grilled goat's cheese on bruschetta, 15
gougère, ratatouille, 88
grapefruit: red mullet with dill and pink grapefruit, 94
Greek raisin roll, 137
Greek-style cheese kebabs, 102
Greek-style lemon fish with potatoes, 39
Gruyère cheese: sweet onion and Gruyère tart, 85

H

halibut: Mediterranean seafood gratinées, 40
ham: hot ham, cheese and garlic baguettes, 134
haricot beans: cassoulet of duckling, 61
garlicky bean and potato casserole, 73
hummus, 16
pasta salad with hummus sesame dressing, 45

I

Italian prawns with pasta, 107
Italian-style fennel with spinach, 84
Italian vegetable soup, 24

K

kebabs: Greek-style cheese kebabs, 102
marinated monkfish, salmon and scallop brochettes, 33
marinated skewered pork with thyme and bay, 70

peppered tomato steak on brochette, 96
spiced pork skewers, 97

L

lamb: French roast lamb with sorrel and watercress stuffing, 67
herbed rack of lamb in a pastry case, 66-7
lamb kibbeh with two dips, 69
Moroccan lamb with apricots, 68
lasagne, aubergine and tomato, 80-1
leafy salad with bacon and brioche croûtons, 46
leek and fennel soup with toast and cheese, 22
lemon: lime and lemon cream dressing, 120
moist lemon honey sponge, 143
preserved lemons and limes, 125
lentils: spiced carrot, lentil and coriander soup, 23
spiced orange chicken with lentils, 52
lime: lime and lemon cream dressing, 120
preserved lemons and limes, 125

M

marinades, 121
mayonnaise, 43, 114-15
meat, 62-72
Mediterranean chicken, 110
Mediterranean chicken pasta with garlic crumbs, 55
Mediterranean seafood gratinées, 40
melon: chicken and melon salad in spiced mayonnaise, 43
microwave recipes, 103-12
mocha pudding with Cointreau cream, 151
monkfish: marinated monkfish, salmon and scallop brochettes, 33

monkfish in aubergine 'cannelloni' with mushroom sauce, 38-39
Moroccan lamb with apricots, 68
Moroccan-style chicken in pastry, 57
Mozzarella cheese: aubergine and tomato Parmigiana, 90
Mozzarella-glazed chicken with aubergine and tomatoes, 51
mushrooms: asparagus, wild mushroom and pine nut risotto, 78
chillied mixed mushrooms, 86
monkfish in aubergine 'cannelloni' with mushroom sauce, 38-39
pancetta-stuffed mushrooms, 92
peppered pork medallions with mushroom crème fraîche, 72
pickled mushrooms in oil, 126
warm salad of mixed mushrooms with garlic croûtons, 10
mussels: paella Valenciana, 79
Portuguese mussel soup, 26
steamed mussels in tomato sauce, 35
mustard dressing, sweet, 116

N

nectarine and crème pâtissière gâteau, 146-7
Normandy-style pork chops, 111
nuts: tipsy apricot, cherry and nut cake, 139

O

olive oil: dried tomatoes in olive oil, 127
goats' cheese marinated in spiced oil, 122
herbed garlic oil, 124
olive oil rolls with sun-dried

tomatoes, 129
paprika oil, 124
pepperoni, 128
pickled mushrooms in oil, 126
olives: marinated artichokes with peppers and olives, 91
marinated spiced olives, 123
roasted mixed peppers with avocado and olive crème fraîche, 13
tapenade, 11
onions: sweet onion and Gruyère tart, 85
walnut and onion bread, 132
oranges: spiced orange chicken with lentils, 52
sunshine fruit and avocado salad, 47

P

paella Valenciana, 79
pan bagna, 135
pancetta-stuffed mushrooms, 92
pancetta-wrapped corn cobs, 99
paprika oil, 124
Parmesan cheese: aubergine and tomato Parmigiana, 90
roasted tomato and garlic soup with Parmesan, 27
veal Parmesan, 65
pasta: Mediterranean chicken pasta with garlic crumbs, 55
pasta and steak in cream sauce, 108-9
pasta salad with hummus sesame dressing, 45
pastries, baklava, 142
pears en brioche, 149
peppered pork medallions with mushroom crème fraîche, 72
peppers: eggs tonnato on pepperoni, 48
marinated artichokes with peppers and olives, 91
peperonata, 103

peppered tomato steak on brochette, 96
pepperoni, 128
Provençal chicken pepper tart, 58
roasted mixed peppers with avocado and olive crème fraîche, 13
roasted sweet peppers with bulgar wheat, 77
rouille, 118
spiced chicken, pepper and lemon couscous, 75
Pernod marinade, 121
pesto, classic basil, 117
pies: spanakhopitas, 17
pizzas: fruit and spice pizza pie, 136
pizza Giorgio, 133
porcini, wine-braised beef with, 62
pork: fruited pork loin, 71
marinated skewered pork with thyme and bay, 70
Normandy-style pork chops, 111
peppered pork medallions with mushroom crème fraîche, 72
spiced pork skewers, 97
Portuguese mussel soup, 26
potatoes: crisp potato skins with soured cream dip, 100
garlicky bean and potato casserole, 73
gratinéed new potatoes with tarragon cream, 87
Greek-style lemon fish with potatoes, 39
sautéed garlic potatoes, 83
prawns: avocado soup with prawn salsa, 20
capellini with prawns, broccoli and red pepper, 82
chargrilled tiger prawns, 95
Italian prawns with pasta, 107
seafood terrine with marinated prawns, 18
Provençal chicken pepper tart, 58

Q

quiches, little Roquefort, 12

R

raisin roll, Greek, 137
ratatouille gougère, 88
red cabbage: ribollita, 28
red mullet with dill and pink grapefruit, 94
red snapper, Greek-style lemon fish with potatoes, 39
ribollita, 28
rice: asparagus, wild mushroom and pine nut risotto, 78
paella Valenciana, 79
Spanish chicken with rice and cabanos, 59
Roquefort cheese: broccoli and Roquefort soup, 29
little Roquefort quiches, 12
Roquefort cheese dressing, 116
toasted walnut, salami and Roquefort salad, 50
rouille, 118

S

salads, 41-50
bitter-sweet duckling salad, 41
chicken and melon salad in spiced mayonnaise, 43
fruited goats' cheese salad, 44
grilled Italian-style salad, 49
leafy salad with bacon and brioche croûtons, 46
pasta salad with hummus sesame dressing, 45
salade Niçoise, 42
sunshine fruit and avocado salad, 47
toasted walnut, salami and Roquefort salad, 50
warm salad of mixed mushrooms with garlic croûtons, 10
salami: toasted walnut, salami and Roquefort salad, 50

salmon: marinated monkfish, salmon and scallop brochettes, 33
baked salmon Florentine en papillote, 30
salt cod: brandade de morue, 19
saltimbocca, 64
sardines, Spanish-style, 36
sauces: rouille, 118
scallops: marinated monkfish, salmon and scallop brochettes, 33
tabbouleh with scallops in a citrus-sharp dressing, 76
seafood: fritto misto di mare, 37
Mediterranean seafood gratinées, 40
mixed seafood with lemony garlic sauce, 11
baked salmon Florentine en papillote, 30
seafood in a filo tart, 32-33
seafood terrine with marinated prawns, 18
sesame seeds: Spanish seeded cornbread, 130
toasted sesame seed dressing, 117
Sicilian-style doughnuts, 150
smoked cod's roe: taramasalata, 16
smoked sausage, mixed bean and vegetable casserole, 74
sole: fritto misto di mare, 37
stuffed sole with cheese and pesto crust, 34
sorrel: French roast lamb with sorrel and watercress stuffing, 67
soups, 20-9
avocado soup with prawn salsa, 20
la bourride, 21
broccoli and Roquefort soup, 29
creamed celery soup with Brie, 106
creamy garlic and chestnut soup, 23

gazpacho, 25
Italian vegetable soup, 24
leek and fennel soup with toast and cheese, 22
Portuguese mussel soup, 26
ribollita, 28
roasted tomato and garlic soup with Parmesan, 27
spiced carrot, lentil and coriander soup, 23
soured cream dip, crisp potato skins with, 100
spanakhopitas, 17
Spanish chicken with rice and cabanos, 59
Spanish seeded cornbread, 130
Spanish-style sardines, 36
spinach: Italian-style fennel with spinach, 84
baked salmon Florentine en papillote, 30
spanakhopitas, 17
starters, 10-19
strawberry cream cheesecake, 140-1
sunshine fruit and avocado salad, 47
swordfish: marinated swordfish cooked in vine leaves, 93

T
tabbouleh with scallops in a citrus-sharp dressing, 76
tagliatelle: Italian prawns with pasta, 107
tagliatelle with a fresh herb and Parmesan sauce, 81
tapenade, 11
taramasalata, 16
tarts: apple frangipane tart, 148-9
glazed fruit tart, 154-5
Provençal chicken pepper tart, 58
seafood in a filo tart, 32-33
sweet onion and Gruyère tart, 85
terrine, seafood with marinated prawns, 18
tomatoes: aubergine and tomato lasagne, 80-1

aubergine and tomato Parmigiana, 90
braised French beans and tomatoes Provençal, 89
crab cakes with tomato salsa, 31
dried tomatoes in olive oil, 127
gazpacho, 25
olive oil rolls with sun-dried tomatoes, 129
peppered tomato steak on brochette, 96
roasted tomato and garlic soup with Parmesan, 27
steamed mussels in tomato sauce, 35
trout: lemony trout with almonds, 109
tuna: eggs tonnato on pepperoni, 48
salade Niçoise, 42
tapenade, 11

V
veal: saltimbocca, 64
veal Parmesan, 65
vegetables, 83-92
barbecued vegetables, 101
Italian vegetable soup, 24
ratatouille gougère, 88
two dips with crudités, 16
vinaigrette, 113
vine leaves, marinated swordfish cooked in, 93

W
walnuts: toasted walnut and chilli dressing, 119
toasted walnut, salami and Roquefort salad, 50
walnut and onion bread, 132
watercress: filo-wrapped Camembert with, 14-15
French roast lamb with sorrel and watercress stuffing, 67
wine marinade, spiced, 121

Y
yogurt dip, minted, 69